Creating Handmade BOOKS

Alisa Golden

Sterling Publishing Co., Inc.
New York

To convert inches to centimeters, multiply by 2.54
To convert inches to millimeters, multiply by 25.4

Designed by Wanda Kossak
All photos by Jim Hair unless otherwise noted

Front cover photo by Nancy Palubniak. From left to right on cover:
painted two-piece box with ginkgo leaf inset; concertina with tabs and
hard wrapped cover with leaf photocopies; single signature with colored
raffia and acrylic inks; chain stitch with painted boards; *Waking Snakes*,
letterpress printed with slot-and-tab structure in a clamshell box; *Up from
Lost*, letterpress printed with side-bound structure and hard cover.

Title page photo of *Onion (ONe I've knOwN)* by Sibila Savage.

Library of Congress Cataloging-in-Publication Data
Golden, Alisa J.
     Creating handmade books/ Alisa Golden.
          p.   cm.
     Includes index.
     ISBN 0-8069-1771-7
     1. Bookbinding. 2. Book design. I. Title.
Z271.G62 1998
686.3-dc21   98-40059
                                                       CIP
               3   5   7   9   10   8   6   4   2

Published by Sterling Publishing Company, Inc.
387 Park Avenue South, New York, N.Y. 10016
© 1998 by Alisa Golden
Distributed in Canada by Sterling Publishing
c/o Canadian Manda Group, One Atlantic Avenue, Suite 105
Toronto, Ontario, Canada M6K 3E7
Distributed in Great Britain and Europe by Cassell PLC
Wellington House, 125 Strand, London WC2R 0BB, England
Distributed in Australia by Capricorn Link (Australia) Pty Ltd.
P.O. Box 6651, Baulkham Hills, Business Centre, NSW 2153, Australia
Printed in China
All rights reserved

Sterling ISBN 0-8069-1771-7

Contents

Simple Adhesive Structures   55

Intermediate Compound Structures   72

Multiple Signatures or Thick Sewn Books   85

Jacob's Ladders   97

Soft and Hard Covers   104

Preface

 was restless. After visiting Berkeley, California, when I was 12, I knew I had to live there. Now I was 19 and unsure of what I would do. After a year and a half of college at the University of California, I dropped out. I had enrolled intending to take art and psychology classes; maybe I would be an art therapist, except I didn't really know what an art therapist did. The therapist idea vaporized; my first psychology class seemed to be just common sense. I also found I didn't like most of the required art courses except the introductory "Form in Color" class with Sylvia Lark. She was a printmaker, and I would have to complete required courses before I could study more with her. I hated the assignments: draw five objects, draw the same still life three ways, make egg tempera, and so on. I was self-absorbed and without a clue. I had an introductory drawing class with Jay DeFeo without knowing who she was; I was unaware of her impact on the art world and her connection to the Beat Generation.

In the fall, I re-enrolled. Before school started, I read Sartre's *Nausea* and I felt detached and disoriented. I hardly made it through the first month before I took down the emergency withdrawal slip that was pinned over my desk, signed it, and dropped out again. I couldn't pick a major. I painted, wrote stories, drew in my journal and carved rubber stamps. I was an artist among intellectuals and among the bureaucracy. I couldn't find my place. Perhaps I should head back to my other creative outlet, I thought.

I went to a guidance counselor, asking if I could sit in on a creative writing class, but was told "it would be disruptive to the class because they establish a rapport and trust each other," or something like that, and would not like a visit from an outsider.

I hung out in cafés, choking back secondhand smoke, and wrote poetry, watching the street people, watching a woman sell her poetry to passersby. I bought a copy of *Writer's Market,* which listed all the names and addresses of poetry publishers. I wrote every day and began sending fiction and poetry to magazines, hoping to get published. *The Berkeley Fiction Review* accepted a story; *The Berkeley Poetry Review* took a poem. A magazine in Australia called *Compass* paid $10 for my poem "Hash Browns & Toast." I felt encouraged even though the rejection slips were piling up much faster than the acceptances.

Meanwhile, I wondered how I could finish my bachelor's degree. Melinda Catlett, my best friend from high school, told me about California College of Arts and Crafts. I went to Oakland, picked up a schedule and read a description of a course taught by Betsy Davids called "Creative Writing and Letterpress Printing." It was a six-unit course, one class for double credit, with printing in the mornings and writing in the afternoon. What piqued my attention was the phrase "merge words and images." In 1983, a student could take classes at CCAC without enrolling in the school. My parents agreed to pay. I went eagerly.

The letterpress class was comfortable and familiar, partly because I had taken a printing shop class in junior high and had learned to set type by hand and print. Betsy was the perfect teacher for me. I didn't want to be told to do anything, and Betsy was reserved and let me explore and work independently, giving me good advice and guidance only when I asked. She taught me the wrapped hard cover, two-sewn-as-one, blockbook binding, accordions with and without flags, and other techniques. I printed a book of the poems I had written in cafés called *never mind the crowd*. When I was done, Betsy said I should press it.

"You mean put it through the press again?" I asked, naively.

"No," she explained gently. "Put it under boards and heavy weights."

Feeling embarrassed and a little silly, I rushed off to wrap the books in waxed paper and put them between Masonite boards with bricks on top to weigh them down until they were dry.

The teaching assistant for that class was Val Simonetti, now a close friend and occasional collaborator. She works carefully and thoughtfully, a balance to my whirlwind approach. I greatly admire both her art and her writing. When I make a book I often think of her as my audience, as if I am creating the book just for her.

I was hooked. I loved printing. I liked to sew and make things. Making books was a way to combine everything I liked to do. When I had writer's block, I could draw; if I didn't know what to draw, I could write. If neither medium inspired me, I could bind a book or design a new one. I could, indeed, merge words and images, which was a relief to me. I applied for admission to CCAC and was accepted, not knowing I had decided my professional career.

I took Betsy's bookmaking class for double credit, plus independent study, and I became her teaching assistant for a year, which firmly planted me in the print shop. Betsy listened to my troubles and helped me with technical problems. She was, and continues to be, my mentor and great support as I found my path and life's work in making books. Her concern about books is that the structure and materials be related to the content. With her partner, Jim Petrillo, working under their imprint, Rebis Press, she incorporated "unusual" materials, such as a shower cap for the book *Half Off* by Mimi Pond, and grommets on canvas covers for a book by Johanna Drucker called *As No Storm or The Anyport Party*. Many bookmakers of the mid-to-late 1970s were much more conservative, focusing on fine printing, and the work of Rebis Press was a bit outside their comprehension. I had a similar reaction to my work from my friends.

she sits on the couch
mouth closed
eyes wide open
face in control
her mind drifting
slowly melting
eyes closing
closing slowly
just a moment
another moment
they close
they open
she knows she's being
watched
knows we're staring
waits for us to look
away
but her eyes
sink
butter eyes
melt
slowly
into
her
cheeks
she wants to
sleep
she wants her
sleep more
than she cares
about the crowd
she doesn't
care about the crowd
she wants a private room
and she knows where
she can get it
suite
suite
dreams

never mind the crowd, 1983, letterpress, photocopy, multiple signatures, 4⁷/₈ x 7"

I took etching and relief printing from Kenneth Rignall; a key-line drawing class from Charles Gill, who was also my advisor; and papermaking, drawing, and silkscreening. Ken showed us how to make clean linoleum cuts and cut out any extraneous material. Charlie stressed precision when making a print. For most printmaking methods you transfer ink from one surface to a piece of paper. Both insisted on clean hands, to avoid smudges on the finished piece. I incorporated each new technique into a new book.

In an ethnic studies silkscreen class Malaquias Montoya talked about content. I could see he hoped we would use our art to improve the world. One student, who was against women in the military, wanted to make a print of a seductive woman model in Army attire with a message, "Is this what you want for your daughter?" and Malaquias told him that he would be reinforcing certain stereotypes if he made that poster. I took Malaquias' words seriously and worked with difficult political topics, trying to evoke a feeling subtly, without blatantly illustrating my point or reinforcing stereotypes.

I did several silkscreen books, including one about the death penalty, entitled *landmind*, and a book about being different or outcast, called *Out. Out.*, before I reluctantly decided that the oil-based process was too toxic (we cleaned the screens with xylene). The school eventually switched to water-based ink, but by then I was making paper and ready to graduate.

I took a papermaking class from Donald Farnsworth. Don once said, "Paper has a memory." I think he meant that paper will dry in a certain shape and stay that way unless dampened again. It also applies to making hard covers or using adhesives; the finished piece must be put under a weight to dry or it will curl. I liked the phrase and used "Paper Has a Memory" as the title for a book in an edition and for a one-of-a-kind book.

The acting president of CCAC at that time was Thomas (Toby) Schwartzburg, who bought several of my books at a school art fair. He gave them to his teenage daughter, Anne, who subsequently took Betsy's class and later became a friend of mine. In 1995, Anne and I collaborated on a book called *Tidal Poems*, in which we both wrote the poems, painted the paper, made linoleum cuts, and letterpress printed the text. I discovered that what makes a good collaboration for me is a combination of two people who work very differently from each other. Anne works slowly and carefully, weighing each decision, yet she can paint wildly and spontaneously. I work quickly and get a great deal done fast, but couldn't paint without thinking methodically about where to put each color. From Anne I learned to loosen up and paint paper freely, something I truly enjoy, find therapeutic, and continue to explore.

landmind, 1984, letterpress, silkscreen, single signature, 11 x 12"

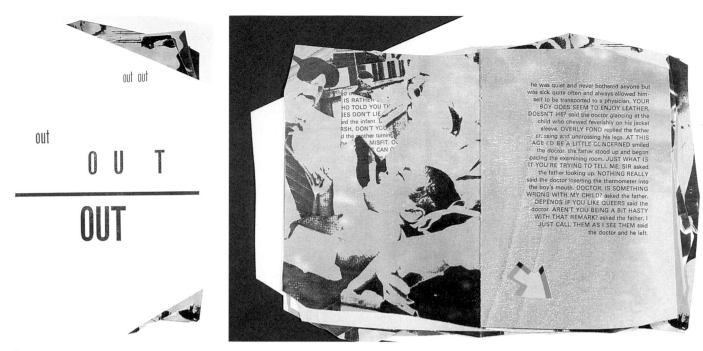

Left: *Out. Out.*, 1984, letterpress, silkscreen, one of five copies, single signature, 5³/₈ x 8"
Right: *Out. Out.* (interior)

For more creative writing guidance I studied with Stephen Ajay. He wrote a phrase on one of my poems that I think of often: "Where are you behind the veils?" When making books I have to constantly touch base with myself so that I'm not just making pretty, interesting books for art's sake.

For a bachelor of fine arts degree I was supposed to have a minor, a certain number of units of a different art form that wasn't printmaking. I was stymied again. I didn't want to do photography or painting, sculpture or anything else. I just wanted to make books. I was irritated; here I was, a writer in an art school. By petitioning the school, I was able to get writing approved as my minor but was told, "this is not to be a precedent for other students." A minor was supposed to enrich your major, but apparently it wasn't supposed to cross certain boundaries.

Thirteen books later, in 1985, I graduated in the top ten, with a B.F.A. in printmaking.

Upon graduating, I joined the Pacific Center for the Book Arts, an organization of which Betsy Davids was a founding member. I was in awe of the professional printers and book artists and a bit afraid of them, but I went to lectures and exhibited in the biennial shows anyway. I became aware

The Hand Correspondence, 1990–1991, Book Two: *Paper Has a Memory*, letterpress, mixed media, single signature with envelope, 4 x 6"

The Dandelion Airplane Book, 1984, letterpress, reduction linoleum cut, single signature, 5 x 6³/₄"

that there was a real community of people who shared my interests.

Still, I had to keep the wolf away from the door. During school I had trained as a typesetter, hoping to make $10 an hour, thinking I might end up as a graphic designer. Briefly, I worked at Wilson Graphics, a company owned by a former mayor of Oakland, typesetting business forms and menus. I set type on a CompuGraphic, a now-obsolete typesetting machine. This was before desktop publishing. I realized I didn't want to be a graphic artist if it meant I would be designing advertisements. I still wanted to improve the world and I didn't think ads would do it. The company folded. Then I sold rub-on letters in the graphic arts department of an art supply store and learned the names of all the typefaces. While working there I met Jim Hair, a photographer, who later took slides of my art. He generously donated his time to take photographs for this book. I also met Pablo Haz, who told me about the Adobe Illustrator program, without which I could not have created the diagrams.

Part-time work allowed me time to continue creating books. I took my first one to a large bookstore in Berkeley. A big guy looked it over.

"Book People picking this up?" he asked. I didn't know that Book People was a distributor. "Well, maybe if they take it, we'll get a couple," he said. Then he looked over the book again and handed it back to me, saying, "I'll pass."

I was mortified. I remembered reading somewhere that you should make a game of it: see how many rejections you could collect. I went to other bookstores.

Later, I sold a few letterpress books on consignment for under $10 each. I sold *The Dandelion Airplane Book*, *A Fish Story*, and *AY*. Edwina Evers (now Leggett) opened Califia Books, an artist's book and fine press bookstore in San Francisco. Val went to work at Califia and became my liaison there. I began to sell my books, not just one or two, but many books. Somebody understood what I was doing and appreciated it. I felt hopeful and surprised. Libraries were adding my books to their collections.

Betsy told me of a printing press that Eileen Callahan, a writer and one of the original members of Five Trees Press, a pioneering women's cooperative, was selling. I bought it. I quit my job, thinking I would print stationery and business cards and invitations for hire. When that didn't work, I went back to work, this time at Pegasus Books, selling used books. Working in the store helped me overcome my intense shyness as I learned to deal with people, a skill necessary for a teacher!

Michael Budiansky and I were married in 1988, and our daughter, Mollie, was born in 1991. When Mollie was three, she showed me a book she was trying to make.

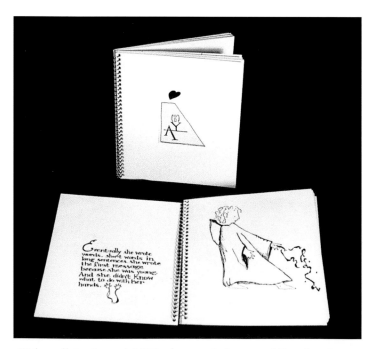

AY (an affair of sorts), 1986, photocopied text and line drawings, commercially done spiral binding, 6 x 6¹/₂"

A Fish Story, 1984, letterpress, linoleum cut, cut-out pages, side-bound, 8³/₄ x 6¹/₂"

"How did you poke the holes?" I asked.

"With a pencil," she replied.

At age seven, Mollie continues to make books, but she only wants to make them *her* way. She doesn't want my help.

Anja Borgstrom, a friend from college, was teaching bookbinding. She called me up and asked me some technical questions. I started asking myself why *I* wasn't teaching, too. Teaching had always made me nervous. I had taught a little but my heart had pounded furiously. I always preferred to be the assistant. I was depressed. I wondered if I should keep making books; I sold some, but not enough to make a living. I decided to be brave and get over my teaching anxiety. Betsy was there again to support me; she brought me in to her classes to give a guest lecture and demonstration.

The Albany Community Center and Library was built in 1994, and I saw an ad saying that they needed teachers; I called them. I was hired without a formal interview. Suddenly, I was a teacher. At the same time, I joined a *dojo* (training hall) and started attending Aikido martial arts classes taught by Elizabeth Lynn two or three times a week. Unconsciously, I patterned my teaching style after her; she was direct and clear, encouraging, and allowed for individual differences. In a book structures class I taught, one insecure student said she would just "take notes and do the binding at home," and I said, "Do the structure now. That's why we're here." In Aikido we were supposed to watch carefully and then do it. We couldn't take notes. The woman was startled, but she put away her notes and made the book.

In 1995, I taught two bookbinding classes through the Extended Education Department at CCAC. My classroom was the "clean room" in the printmaking department, a comfortable place I knew from 10 years before. I had some younger and very quiet students as well as 35- to 50-year-old women. All seemed eager to make hardcover books and boxes but not that anxious to do the more unusual structures. This attitude seemed strange in an art school. For the second class, I had students cut words out of magazines and make poems or sentences with the words. The students were so engaged in this activity, we didn't have time to finish. I had hoped to teach a combined writing and bookbinding class but was told by the administration that nobody would take it. Adding an "artistic" way of writing to the book structures class seemed to work.

I watched Judith Tannenbaum, a poet in residence, teach high school students; she was firm, but she didn't try to control them. Judith had taken my class and afterwards brought me in as a guest to teach bookbinding to kids. When I came to one class, three of the kids wouldn't join us at the table but sat in chairs as far away as possible. But, as I taught, I saw that they were interested in what we were doing and did make each of the books. I thought back to how Betsy had given me room to think for myself, just as I saw Judith do with the high school students. It worked. It was okay to let students explore; they didn't have to bind a book exactly the same way I was doing it.

I learned how to be more attentive to individual needs when I went with Lisa Kokin to teach adults at two homeless shelters. Lisa is a Berkeley artist who has exhibited internationally. She works with found objects and makes one-of-a-kind books and objects. She received a grant from the California Arts Council to teach art to the homeless, and she brought me in as a guest teacher. In this book I include anecdotes about our classes together.

he has always been this way. dark clothes he likes especially. dark pants, sweaters, and socks to match. he doesn't talk. he doesn't say much. he never learned that to meet people he must ask them questions or talk about himself. he wouldn't know what questions to ask them. well, there are alot of questions in his head, but he doesn't ask them. he never asks. and as for talking about himself, well, that's his own business. he likes his privacy.

Left: *Reason: Independence, Privacy.* 1983, letterpress, silkscreen, die-cut pages, single signature, 8 x 9$^{1}/2$"
Right: *Reason: Independence, Privacy.* Interior.

Lisa stood by one elderly man and guided him each step of the way. Although the structure was repetitive, he lost track of what he was doing after each step. "Now fold this paper. Get your glue stick. Put glue on the back. Line it up. Press it down," etc. When he completed the structure he asked what to do next. I suggested he could write things in his book, such as names and addresses, or anything else he might like. He asked for a pencil, then wrote in a shaky hand, "Mine sons and daughter." He listed his six sons, all beginning with the same letter, and his one daughter. By making a book with us the man received our attention, attention that his family was clearly not giving him. Maybe we were doing art therapy, after all.

I joined the Board of Directors of the Pacific Center for the Book Arts and organized a series of salonlike gatherings patterned after some private meetings that Anna Wolf had held. I wanted more book artists to meet and see one another's work up close. I wanted new people to feel welcomed into the community and not be intimidated. Each evening three artists gave half-hour presentations and answered questions. About 30 people showed up every couple of months. These artists' works and their stories were inspiring.

Meanwhile, our growing daughter was making the house feel smaller and smaller; it was harder for me to work in the tiny, eight-foot-square office Michael and I shared. We had a studio built in 1995, where I continue to teach letterpress and bookbinding workshops.

I discovered that my neighbor, Nan Wishner, was a poet and writing teacher. I knew I wanted to help my students merge writing and making books, but I was frustrated. I wrote, but I didn't know how to teach writing. I had always thought that if you wanted to write, you just wrote. But it wasn't that easy. Upon talking further with Nan, I found her bursting with ideas about writing. She opened a window for me: there was more than one creative way to teach writing! I was excited. We team-taught some classes together, generating words onto paper, then binding them into a book. After a workshop the students would exclaim, "I can write!" One said, "I didn't know it could be so easy!" Nan got the students to write without being afraid that their writing wasn't "good enough." She became my friend; by proofreading this book and asking certain questions, she helped me open up parts of myself I had closed unknowingly. I hope I will be able to give my students the same gifts.

In 1997, Michael and I had a son, Ezra. He currently eats books.

I taught many classes at the Community Center. For each class I taught I prepared a manual of instructions. Michael said, "You should write a book of those." I said, "I am." He said, "No, a *real* book." Well, here it is.

Introduction

ake one piece of paper and a pair of scissors, and you have the tools to create a book. Add a needle and thread, a pot of glue, and a brush and you can make a variety of structures. Tell a family story, rubber-stamp a poem, use photographs in sequence, and the book becomes vibrant and alive. Even if you want to make a hardcover book, you must still start by folding paper.

This is an introduction to bookbinding structures. I include simple structures and compound structures that are combinations of one or more simple ones. I also include a few complex and more elaborate bindings. I emphasize working with archival materials that will remain strong and that will not yellow over time.

Think of the books you create using these directions as your samples. At first they will be blank. When you feel comfortable doing your own binding or when you feel inspired, you can start to "work from the inside, out." This can mean finding or creating words and images first, then binding them into a book, or finding out what is inside yourself that needs to be

Left: Paper, scissors, book
Right: Back to front: *Talking Alphabet, Onion, Mrs. White Has Tea, Buddha's Bowl, Tree Gets a Ticket Left*

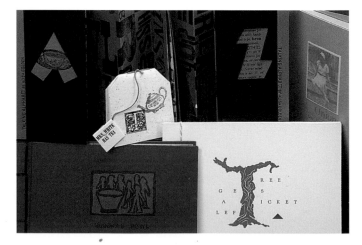

expressed, and working out how to express it clearly and appropriately. While any of the structures can be used to tell any story, ideally the binding and materials should relate to and enhance the contents, helping to make the meaning clear. For my art-by-mail series, *The Hand Correspondence*, I put three books into three handmade envelopes and mailed them to buyers. The stamps and buyers' names became part of the art, which was about communication.

When pages are bound into a permanent structure, the sequence also becomes fixed. Fiction, nonfiction, and series of images that clearly have a narrative are most easily read in bound form. You may find that a certain structure suggests specific contents.

One-of-a-kind objects are considered valuable, and therefore their creation tends to produce fear in the beginner. In our culture we are afraid to be beginners, afraid of making mistakes. Put aside this fear if you can, and let your hands work for you. The more mistakes you make, the more you learn.

When you decide to create a book, as a gift or for practice, make more than one. You will be more relaxed knowing you have a backup if you make a mistake. Binding additional books will also improve your craft.

Musicians practice every day, and painters paint every day. The Impressionists painted the same scenes at different times of day and different times of year until they finally began to know their subjects. Writers write. Binders bind. The more times you create a book, the better you will

The Hand Correspondence, 1990–1991, letterpress, mixed media, tied bundle of three books in envelopes, 4 x 6"

Left: *The Hand Correspondence*, 1990–1991, letterpress, mixed media, three books in envelopes, 4 x 6"
Right: *The Hand Correspondence*, 1990–1991, Book Three: *Voyeur*, letterpress, mixed media, single signature with envelope, 4 x 6"

understand what makes a workable structure. Eventually, with practice, you will be able to design your own binding to suit your specific project.

The following structures are arranged from simple to complex so that you can exercise and build your skills as you go.

Choosing Size

Most of the structures in this book can be created from sheets of $8^{1}/_{2}$ x 11" paper, since not everyone has a paper cutter at home or the resources to buy fine printmaking paper. Once you make a structure with which you are satisfied using standard copy paper, you may want to make a book from different paper and of a different size. The appendix of this book lists the suggested weight and type of paper for each project.

Before you begin to make a book, determine the paper you will use. Then decide if the book should be small, medium, or large. Smaller books are from over 3" to a maximum of 6–8". Whatever you can hold in your hand and still turn its pages is considered a small book. These are the most intimate and are good for personal subjects. Books smaller than 3" square are called miniature books and are often sought by collectors. Medium-size books can be held in the lap and shared with another person. Large books I think of as being suitable for public and political subjects. They are read on a table or displayed in a case. Many people can view them at once.

Once you have decided on miniature, small, medium, or large, divide a sheet of paper into halves, quarters, and eighths. See if one of these sizes works, which will avoid wasting paper. Some standard sizes of fine art papers are 18 x 24" (drawing paper, colored—but not construction—paper), 22 x 30" (most heavier, printmaking papers), 27 x 35" (Asian papers, which some people call rice paper, although the paper contains no rice whatsoever).

Tools List

Some basic tools are necessary to make the structures in this book. You will find more detailed descriptions of these items in subsequent chapters.

For Marking and Scoring

pencil

18" or 24" metal ruler or metal-edged ruler

bone folder—a wide, flat stick with one pointed end for creasing paper and making grooves in the paper to aid folding (It is often sold with the burnishers in the graphic arts section of art supply stores. A butter knife or thumbnail also works.)

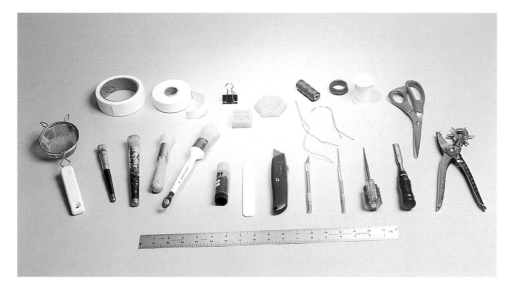

Tools: Top row (left to right): self-adhesive linen tape, gummed reinforcement tape, binder clip, two cakes of beeswax, bookbinding needle, curved needle, waxed linen macrame/basketmaking thread, linen thread, scissors. Middle row: strainer, four stencil brushes, glue stick, bone folder, utility knife, X-Acto knife, needle tool, awl, woodworker's wedge, rotating leather punch. Bottom row: metal ruler

For Cutting

scissors

#1 art knife and extra #11 blades, or other small, sharp knife and extra blades

utility knife, craft knife, or mat knife and new blades, for cutting boards

cutting mat (any color self-healing cutting mat) or layers of cardboard

fine-grain sandpaper (to smooth the rough edges of cut boards)

For Sewing

awl, bodkin (clay "needle" tool), or drill with tiny bit and vise/clamp

needle (a bookbinding needle is stronger and has a smaller eye that is less likely to break)

curved needle (for chain stitch)

thread (linen, poly-wrapped cotton, or anything that doesn't stretch or break when pulled)

beeswax, to wax thread (makes thread less likely to tangle and helps hold the knots more tightly)

rotating punch (Commonly used for punching holes in leather, it has several sizes of holes and can be found at a hardware store.)

1 binder clip (medium)

For Gluing

wheat paste powder

stainless steel strainer (strains lumps out of paste)

Polyvinyl acetate (PVA) glue

wide-mouthed plastic containers (such as cottage cheese containers)

stencil brush, large size (flat bottom, 1–2" round diameter, make sure bristles are firmly attached)

pages from glossy magazines or catalogues for scrap paper (Use plenty, so you can have a new, clean surface every time you glue something. Use glossy paper, because the ink will not transfer to your project. Do *not* use newspaper.)

heavy book (Use as a weight to flatten your book while it is drying.)

waxed paper (to put on either side of your book as a barrier between glued parts and the weight used for drying; also to put between glued end-sheets and the dry book block)

wood glue (for scroll knobs)

The following materials are optional:

woodworker's wedge tool

12 x 16" Masonite boards (smooth on two sides, to use between books or covers that were glued and need to be dried flat)

self-adhesive linen tape (for the circle accordion structure)

bookbinder's cloth tape in different colors (for portfolios)

gummed reinforcement tape (to cover joins inside box corners)

polymer clay for making buttons or clasps (i.e., Sculpey, Fimo)

varnish for the polymer clay

bone clasps

raffia (A strawlike cord, it comes in a natural tan and in other colors; for sewing side-bound books, ledgers, and for stick binding.)

waxed linen macramé thread in various colors

rubber-stamp alphabet

stamp pads (I like ColorBox brand; they are pigmented and permanent.)

plastic or artgum erasers

ribbon

acrylic paints

acrylic gel medium

gesso

acrylic inks

pigmented archival marking pens

Some Basic Terms

Accordion: paper folded to have alternating peak and valley folds; also called concertina

Artist's book: a book made by a person who likes to make art. The artist controls the work from start to finish, making all the decisions about text, binding, illustrations, and design.

Book arts: an all-encompassing term used to describe bookbinding, paper-making, paper marbling, calligraphy, letterpress printing, etc. I tend to use the singular, "book art," when I talk about handmade books; I use it interchangeably with "artist's book" or "artists' books."

Book block: the group or stack of text papers, sewn or glued together, usually without covers

Edition: formally, a group of identical, multiple copies of a book that are signed and numbered by the author and artist/illustrator. These books are called an "edition." You can vary the books as you make them; there are no book-art police.

Endpapers or endsheets: the papers at the front and back of the book, sometimes glued to the cover as well; usually decorative

Fore edge: the side of the book that opens, usually parallel to the spine

Head: the top edge of the book when it is lying flat on a table

Landscape orientation: paper or book placed in front of you horizontally

One-of-a-kind: a book that is not part of an edition, but the only one you make; also called a "unique book"

Peak fold: a fold that makes a mountain

Running stitch: sewing in one hole and out the immediate neighboring hole

Score: to draw an indentation in the paper. It helps to make a straight fold. Scoring also allows heavier paper to crease without rough edges.

Side-bound: a Japanese style of binding in which holes are punched along one edge of a stack of pages, and then bound with cord, thread, or ribbon. I use the terms stab-binding, blockbook binding, and Japanese side-binding interchangeably.

Signature: a group or gathering of folded pages that nest, one inside the other

Single signature: one group of folded, nested pages sewn together to create a pamphlet; also called **pamphlet stitch**

Spine: the side of the book where the pages are bound together; also the part that shows when the book is closed and on a shelf

Tail: the bottom edge of the book

Turn-ins: where the cover is folded over boards and usually glued

Valley fold: a fold that makes a groove

About the Times

The times indicated for making each structure are approximate. They do not include the time it takes to cut the paper to size, prepare to work, or decorate the paper.

About the Diagrams

The diagrams illustrate key steps for making books. A solid line shows the edge of the paper or a previous fold. A line of long dashes indicates a valley fold. A line of short dashes indicates a peak fold. You may have to re-fold a valley fold into a peak fold; watch the diagrams. When you need to adhere something, the gray line indicates glue or paste. Arrows show the direction you should sew, where something will go, or if you need to turn the paper over.

————	EDGE
✂————	CUT
– – – – – – ·	VALLEY FOLD
· · · · · · · · ·	PEAK FOLD
～～～～	GLUE
↶↴	TURN OVER

CHAPTER 1

Cut and Folded Books

With a cut or series of punches or slits, you can transform a piece of paper into a book. This idea seems simple, yet I discovered most of these structures years after I learned the more complicated, traditional bookmaking techniques. I have little bits of folded paper all over my desk from trying new approaches. After you learn a few techniques by heart, keep a stack of paper by the telephone. Instead of doodling, practice folding, to improve this basic skill. Before you begin any of the projects in this book, please read the instructions carefully.

A Note on Paper

Most papers have a grain, or a direction in which they would more naturally curl. In making books, grain should always run parallel to the spine so that the paper can be folded easily and to prevent warping.

To find the direction of the grain: balance a piece of paper on your arm lengthwise, then balance it widthwise. In one of these ways the paper will curl more naturally. You can also fold the paper lightly each way without creasing it. Whichever way the paper bends more easily is the direction of the grain. If the grain is parallel to the longest side of the paper, we say it is grained long. To understand about paper grain, tear a piece of newspaper first one way then the other, to see which yields a straight, not ragged, edge. The grain is parallel to the straight edge. Some Japanese and hand-made papers have no distinguishable grain.

Photocopy papers are usually grained long, in other words, parallel to the longest side of the paper. Some business paper or fine stationery is often grained short or parallel to the short edge of the paper. At business and stationery supply stores you may be able to check the grain on a sample sheet before you buy.

Always cut your paper so the grain is parallel to the spine. Cut all boards and papers so the grain runs in the same direction; this is especially important when you begin using adhesives. When the boards and papers become wet with glue, they will curl along the grain and dry that way if they are not flattened while drying. If you glue two pieces of paper with mismatched, or crossed, grain, each will pull in a different direction and the finished project will be warped.

Cutting Paper

By Hand

We learn to use scissors at an early age; therefore, most people are comfortable with them. When cutting paper for more complicated books, however, scissors can yield an imprecise cut. They are also not practical for cutting large quantities of paper or heavy board. It is much better to cut a precise line with the very sharp blade of a small art knife. So, in addition to scissors, you will need a small knife and blades, a metal ruler, and cardboard or a self-healing mat to protect your work surface and prolong the life of your blade.

Always cut against a metal ruler or straightedge because plastic and wood can be nicked easily, which will give you a wobbly cut. Cork-backed rulers don't slip, but be aware of the extra thickness from the cork. Since the cork does not extend to the edge, a cork-backed ruler is slightly unstable. If you do not press firmly on the ruler, your knife can slip underneath it, and if you press on the edge of the ruler you risk slicing your fingers. You can also put masking tape on the back of a ruler for extra traction. Work on top of cardboard or a self-healing cutting mat to protect your furniture and to keep your knife blade from getting dull too fast. I find it easier to cut while standing. I can get a good angle, see what I'm doing, maintain even pressure, and make a cut in one stroke.

A mat knife or utility knife, also with a new or sharp blade, is preferable for cutting stacks of paper and boards. You can tell your blade is getting dull if the board doesn't cut all the way through the first time or has a ragged edge. If you do have a ragged edge, the tiny tip of your blade has probably broken off. In all cases, keep your fingers on top of the ruler, not over the edge!

Purchasing a Paper Cutter

When you find yourself cutting paper for many books or for books with many pages, you may consider purchasing a paper cutter. Two kinds are sold in art supply and office supply stores. One has a long, large blade that chops the paper. The other has a sliding or rotating blade that slits the paper, much like a handheld knife. Some cutters have a self-sharpening blade, and sometimes the blades are small and easy to replace without worrying about proper alignment.

I use a large 24" chopper, and a lightweight 12" cutter with interchangeable, rotating blades. The standard blade makes a straight cut; the fancy blades make zigzags, perforations, scallops; one even scores paper without cutting it. The small cutter cannot cut boards. The large chopper is excellent for cutting large, heavy-weight paper. To cut boards, it's necessary sometimes to push tightly on them, to prevent them from pulling or shifting as the blade comes down and making a diagonal cut. It helps to pull the handle of the chopper in toward the boards as you bring it down.

Board cutters are also available. If you find yourself making lots of boxes or hardcover books, consider one. They come in a variety of sizes and prices with either a 45-degree angled/beveled head or a 90-degree head (you'll want the latter for books and boxes). I find I can measure and cut by hand adequately with a mat knife and a long metal ruler.

Whether you choose a chopping cutter or a slicing one, a ruler printed directly on the cutter is extremely useful. You can measure and cut at the same time, leaving less chance for error.

Folding Paper

The man standing at the end of the table at a Berkeley homeless shelter hesitated for a moment, unsure about joining the free art class. "I'm not an artist," he said. I said we were just folding paper. He sat down. He folded paper with us and made a book. He seemed pleased.

Fold paper by matching two corners and aligning the edge that is perpendicular to the fold you are about to make. With the side of your hand or a bone folder, smooth and crease from the corner diagonally toward the fold. Work progressively toward the top of the paper. Folding paper by aligning it this way takes into account that the paper may not be perfectly square when you begin. This could be due to a misaligned paper cutter or a hasty mistake by the paper manufacturer.

Any size bone folder is helpful to make a tight, neat crease. But you can use other tools, such as a wooden spoon. A bone folder is a smooth, flat, wide stick. Bone folders used to be made of whalebone. Nowadays, they are made of cow bone or hard plastic. Bone folders have either two rounded ends, or one rounded end and one pointed end. The point is great for scoring paper. You can resharpen the point by sanding it or filing the edges.

Scoring Paper

Score paper by marking it lightly at the top and bottom with a very sharp pencil (a dull pencil can yield a wide mark, which can interfere with your careful measurements). Line up a ruler to the marks; and, with the pointed end of the bone folder, your thumbnail, or butter knife, press a line into the paper.

Hidden Book
(folding and cutting)

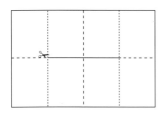

Time: 5–10 minutes

A three-dimensional book is hidden in every piece of paper. *Earthwords* uses this one-page format and has a printed collage on the back which is only slightly visible to the reader, yet the book can be opened to view the complete picture.

Materials: 8½ x 11" paper, scissors or knife, self-healing cutting mat, metal ruler, bone folder

1. Fold a piece of paper in half lengthwise. Open.
2. Fold in half widthwise. Open.
3. Turn the paper over so the widthwise fold becomes a peak.
4. Fold in the ends to the widthwise fold. Open. You have just made an accordion fold.
5. Cut a slit down the lengthwise fold only along the middle two sections.
6. Fold in half again lengthwise.
7. Push the ends together so the middle section will make an X, and then form pages.
8. Fold over the middle sections and wrap around to make book.

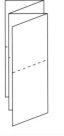

step 5

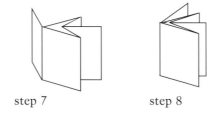

step 6

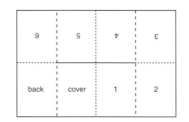

step 7   step 8

6	5	4	3
back	cover	1	2

All printing or writing can be done on one side of a piece of paper, before it is folded up. (See the diagram for how the pages are oriented.) Or, draw a scene on the back of the paper using the middle four sections (two sections right-side up, two upside-down). For my sister Nina's 31st birthday I made a scene of an ice cream store in the middle, making up 31 fictitious flavors, each relevant to a part of her life. I cut windows so the scene was partially visible when the book was closed.

Uses: birthday card, greeting card, one poem

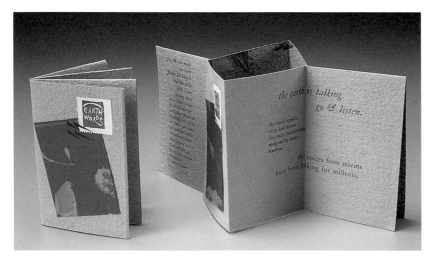

Earthwords, 1995, letterpress, hidden book, 4 x 5" (photo by Sibila Savage)

Simple Accordion
(folding) from rectangular paper

Time: 5 minutes

The middle of this book has one fold across the top. By opening the book from various directions (back, front, side, and other side), you can use four different texts like *Talking Alphabet*. I added a single signature at the fold.

Materials: rectangular paper, scissors or knife, straightedge or metal ruler, cutting mat, bone folder

1. Fold paper in half, lengthwise. Open.
2. Fold in half, widthwise. Open.
3. Turn over so the widthwise fold becomes a peak.
4. Fold in the ends to the widthwise fold. Open.
5. Cut down the lengthwise fold, leaving one rectangle from the edge. Accordion-fold, alternating peaks and valleys.

Variation: Sew a single signature (see page 49) in the horizontal fold in the center of the book.

Uses: greeting card, change of address, text describing points of view
   I used this structure in a personal, one-of-a-kind book called *Date Book* for my parents' 35th anniversary. I did little collages and used bits of the stories they had told me about how they met. At the fold I made a pop-up. I gave them the book inside a paper portfolio which had the letter "G" stamped in sealing wax.

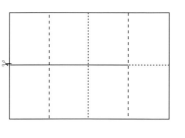

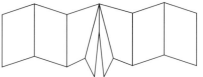

step 5

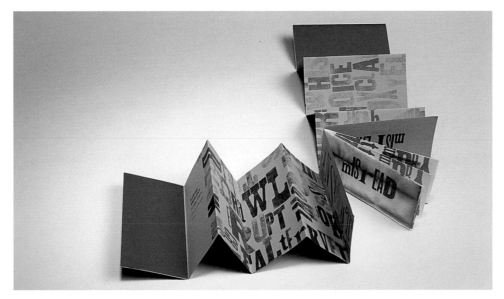

Talking Alphabet, 1994, letterpress, simple accordion with single signature, 3³/₈ x 6¹/₄"

Simple Accordion with Tunnel
(folding and cutting) from rectangular paper

Time: 10–25 minutes

This simple, folded book makes an enchanting dioramalike structure when fully opened. Ed Hutchins likes this structure and sent me a couple of his books that use it, *The Forgotten Closet* and *San Francisco, 1969*, which has cutouts of a cable car, Coit tower, and the Golden Gate Bridge. *When Again Was* is my first simple accordion with a tunnel. You can find more of this structure in *A Book of One's Own*, by Paul Johnson.

Materials: rectangular paper, scissors or a small sharp knife, straightedge or metal ruler, cutting mat, bone folder

1. Fold the paper in half, lengthwise. Open.
2. Turn over.
3. Fold in half widthwise. Open.
4. Turn over.
5. Fold in the ends to the widthwise fold. Open.
6. Cut down the lengthwise fold, leaving one rectangle from the edge.
7. Cut diamonds or ovals in A, B, C, each one smaller than the one before. (When you pick images for this book, you will cut shapes to match the contour of the images; the diamonds or ovals are just for the sample book.)
8. Fold A, B, C, D, the top row of rectangles, in an accordion pattern (alternating peak and valley).
9. Fold the closed pages down over the last rectangle (H).
10. Accordion-fold E, F, G, H.

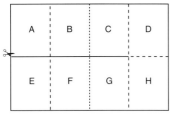

step 6

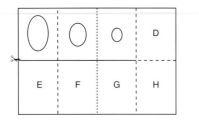

step 7

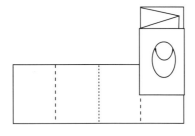

step 8

When Again Was, 1997, color photocopy edition, tunnel accordion, 2³/₄ x 4¹/₄"

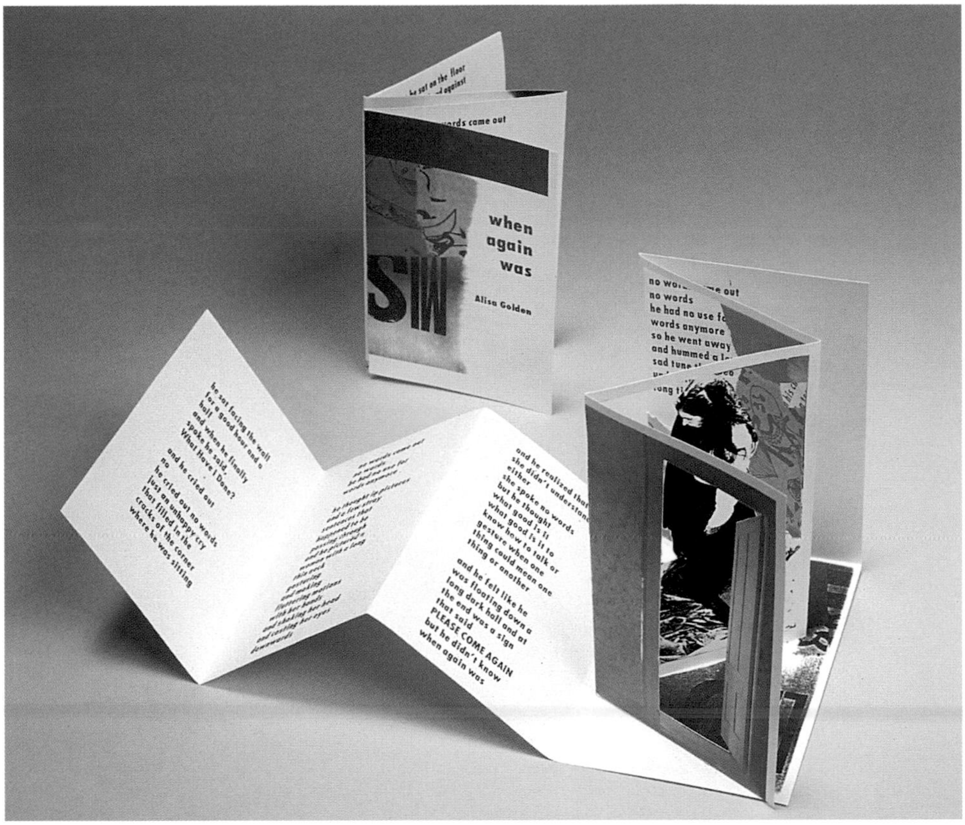
when
again
was
Alisa Golden

When Again Was (open)

The bottom row of rectangles becomes the main body of the book. The top row is folded forward instead of back like the plain, simple accordion. It makes a flap that, when open, becomes the tunnel, sitting zigzag on the far-right bottom rectangle.

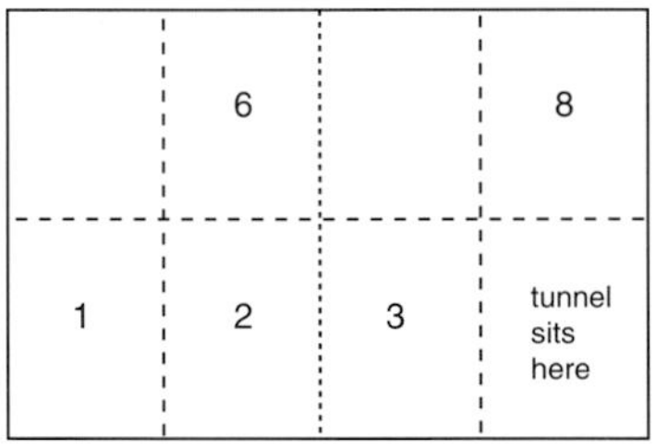
6
8
1
2
3
tunnel sits here

side 1

Choosing images: You may choose to use all of the same picture, cutting out different elements for a sculptural effect. Or pick or create four unique, vertical images.

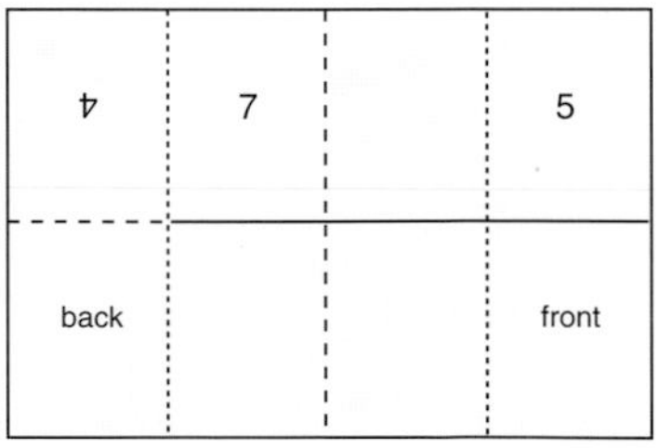
4
7
5
back
front

side 2

1. The first image should be mostly cut away (a big open window, gate, door, or other frame).
2. The next picture should also be able to stand out with space around it.
3. The third has less cut out.
4. The last will not be cut at all, but needs to be able to be seen through the preceding pages.

Variation #1: Use a color photocopy on one side and a black-and-white photocopy on the other (see the diagram for placement of images and text).
Variation #2: Draw a pattern of triangles on page H to indicate where the tunnel sits up perpendicular to the far-right rectangle.

Uses: family greeting card, presentation of a single poem

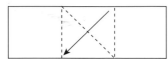

Twist Card

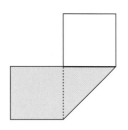

Time: 5–10 minutes

For the book arts exhibit *Art and Soul of the Handmade Book* in Vashon Island, Washington, Catherine Michaelis and Beth Dunn used this structure for the announcement/keepsake. It reminded me that I had first seen it in *Creative Cards*: *Wrap a Message with a Personal Touch*, by Yoshiko Kitagawa. Using two sheets of paper gives it a more booklike feel because you can turn the pages.

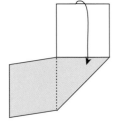

step 7

Materials: two pieces of contrasting rectangular paper (the length is three times the height: use 9 x 3", for example), ruler, pencil, bone folder, decorative-edge scissors (optional)

1. Place one piece of paper horizontally in front of you.
2. Measure one third from the right or left edge.
3. Score and fold.
4. Flip paper over and fold the other edge over to the fold. Line up exactly and crease. You should have one peak and one valley fold that divide the paper into three even sections.
5. Open the paper completely and refold one fold so you have two valley folds.

step 8

6. Repeat with the second color of paper, and nest inside the first to match up the folds.
7. Align one of the straight valley folds across the paper to the perpendicular edge. This action puts a crease diagonally across the middle section. You will see one color square and another color square connected to a triangle.
8. Fold the contrasting square back over the triangle.
9. Turn the paper over. Now you will see two contrasting triangles.

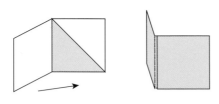

step 9   step 10

10. Fold up the other square over the triangles to make a neat square.

Variation #1: As added decoration, after you are finished cut a zigzag or decorative edge on each of the two papers at opposite ends.

Variation #2: You can also make this structure freehand, without measuring, as long as the proportions are the same as above. Stack the two papers, tops and bottoms aligned, slightly staggered left and right. Fold them together into thirds, freehand, the way you would fold a business letter. Then proceed with step #7.

Uses: birth announcement, birthday card (fold up a check or money inside)

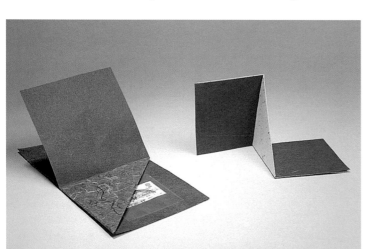

Twist cards, 1997, sample card, 3 x 3", with postage stamp, 4 x 4"

House Card

Time: 5–10 minutes

My daughter Mollie brought this structure home from her first-grade class. The children drew pictures of themselves and their families on each of the open flaps. Anne Hiller, the teacher, didn't remember where she had learned it. I added signatures sewn into the valley folds when I made *A Certain Curtain*.

Materials: one sheet of rectangular paper (you can use two color photocopies on one side that fill up the paper, one right-side-up and the other upside-down)

step 1

steps 2 and 3

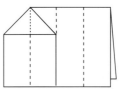

step 4

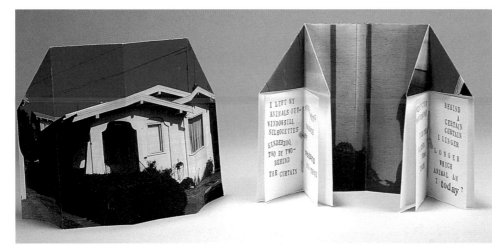

A Certain Curtain, 1997, color photocopy and rubber stamps, 5¹/₂ x 8¹/₂" (open)

1. Fold the paper in half, widthwise. (If you are using color photocopies, make sure the color is on the peak side; in other words, start with the white side up.)

2. Keeping the paper folded, fold it again, this time into quarters; then open it.

3. Fold the top and bottom edge into the middle. You will have three valley folds on this side.

4. Put your thumb under the edge at the top fold and pull the paper down while folding in the valley fold. When the paper edge aligns with the center fold, crease two diagonals to make a triangular shape.

5. Repeat on other side.

6. To put this into an envelope, fold in the outside ends on the existing folds to make the house into a rectangle. You may wish to fold it once again on the existing folds to make a small, compact booklike object.

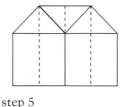

step 5

step 5

step 6

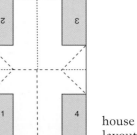

house layout

Variation: Sew a single signature into the front and back folds. (See page 50 for instructions.)

Uses: housewarming invitation, thank-you note, open-house invitation, birth announcement

Palm Leaf Book
(punching and threading)

Time: 15–30 minutes

In college, Betsy took our bookmaking class to the Bancroft Library at University of California, Berkeley, where I saw an authentic palm leaf book; the text was inscribed on real palm leaves.

Materials: cards or heavy paper (such as 2-ply museum board or Lenox 100, Rives BFK) cut into 14 or more 1½ x 5" strips, pencil, ruler, small hole punch (can be a diamond or any shape), waxed macramé cord or other somewhat thick, durable string (approximately 2' long)

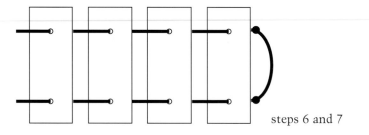

steps 6 and 7

1. Cut the paper into strips, 1½ x 5".
2. Measure one strip at 1" from each long end, centered.
3. With your small hole punch, punch a hole at each end, 1" from the edge.
4. Use this card as a template to line up all the holes. Don't try to punch the rest through the template: use a pencil to draw lines through it.
5. Measure out about two feet of the cord. Make a knot at 6" from the end. Begin threading through the top holes of all the cards.
6. When you get to the last one, make another knot, leaving room for the cards to turn but not to flatten out.
7. Make another knot the same measurement as the distance between the holes. Then continue threading through the bottom holes. Make the last knot leaving a 6" tail.
8. The book should be able to "open"; that is, the pages should be able to move snugly but not be too cramped, and loose enough but not so loose as to be unwieldy. It should probably be able to sit up in a V shape. To close, simply pull and tie ends together in a bow.

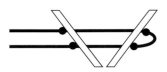

step 8

Variation #1: You may choose to put large beads on each of these ends and knot again. The two or more beads should be larger than the hole.

Variation #2: Use acrylic paint and gel medium. Use two colors that will mix well. Paint the paper before you cut it down into strips as follows: Put out a blob of paint onto a piece of scrap paper or small palette. With a stencil or large, short-bristled dry brush, work the paint onto the paper, both colors, blending a little. It should dry very fast. Repeat for the other side. If the paint feels dry to you, do not add water (this may warp your paper); thin with the gel medium instead. To prevent cards from sticking, mix colors with white gesso. (The colors will be pastel-like and not as vibrantly bright.)

Variation #3: Rubber-stamp with a poem or invitation before assembling.

Variation #4: Collage the cards before assembling with photocopies of family members or friends.

Variation #5: Cut the strips into shapes (such as leaves or fish), then punch and thread.

Variation #6: Leave enough cord so the book flattens out, creating an effect like a game, when all the cards are spread out.

Uses: guest book (each guest signs one leaf). Make a book about trees, fishing, a series of things connected (palm reading or family ties).

Tall Green Grass or *Tickling Your Palm*, 1995, acrylics and rubber stamps, palm leaf book, 2 x 6¹/₂"

Venetian Blind Book
(punching and threading)

Time: 10 minutes

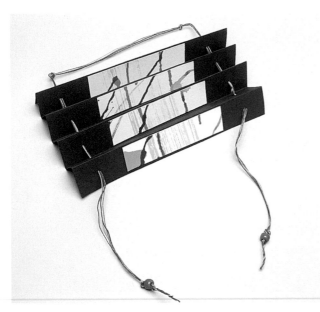

Venetian Blind Book, 1997, acrylic inks, waxed linen, glass beads, 1¹/₄ x 8"

I put a tiny Venetian blind in *Mirror/Error*, Book One in *The Hand Correspondence*. The text was about seeing into a window and watching a couple interact.

Don't be afraid, but precision is important here.

Materials: Medium-weight paper 5" x 20", grained short; awl, ice pick or bodkin; macramé cord or other somewhat thick, durable string (approximately two lengths of 20" each or 1¹/₄ yards total); ruler; pencil

side view

To make the basic accordion with eight sections:

1. Fold the paper in half widthwise with the grain parallel to the fold. Open.
2. Fold the edges in to the fold.
3. Fold the edges back to the new folds, aligning them.
4. Turn the paper over. Take the folded edges and align them with the middle fold, and crease.
Then:
5. Measure approximately one inch from each end. Mark. Fold up.
6. With your awl, punch through the folded accordion, putting cardboard underneath, in order not to damage your work surface.
7. Repeat at the other end.
8. Tie a knot on one of the 20" cords, 2" from the end.
9. Thread through all the top holes.
10. Tie another knot, leaving another 2".
11. Repeat for the other cord/end.
12. To close, pull the strings tightly, pushing the accordion together. Tie the ends together in a bow or make a loose slip knot, using both cords in the same knot. Trim the ends first, if necessary.

Variation #1: Cut a photograph or photocopy into four strips slightly narrower than the accordions and smaller than the distance between the two holes. Glue down to every other edge. (A glue stick works well with thin papers.)

Variation #2: Paint thin watercolor paper first with acrylic inks. Let dry and proceed as above.

Variation #3: With pigmented marking pens, write a four-line poem or other text on every other accordion.

Variation #4: Use one long cord (like the one in the photograph).

Uses: birthday card, sympathy card, short poem about windows

Simple Pop-Up Card

Time: 10–15 minutes

With a few cuts you can make a piece of paper pop up to become three-dimensional. Fold a piece of paper in half, draw a shape centered exactly on the fold, then cut precisely around the outside of the shape, leaving the right and left edges still attached. By refolding the valley fold to a peak fold, you create a pop-up.

Sunflowers in December & Sunflowers for Sale or Rent, 1995, interior pop-up from *A Garden Variety Book*, Book Three, letterpress, linoleum cut, 3¹/₂ x 5¹/₂"

After you experiment with simple shapes, try rubber-stamping or photocopying in the middle of the page and cutting around the edges, leaving a generous margin and two spots where the picture is attached. To learn some more elaborate and wonderful pop-up techniques, see *The Pop-Up Book*, by Paul Jackson.

Carol Barton and Dorothy Yule are masters of the pop-up, often using two or more "pops" in a single image. I admire their intricate work. Carol lives in Maryland and curates shows and teaches. She is the co-author and curator of *Books & Bookends*, the catalog for a traveling exhibit of the same name. Her work can also be seen in *Cover to Cover*, by Shereen LaPlantz. Dorothy is based in Berkeley and sells her work at Califia Books, in San Francisco. Both have books in special collections departments of libraries around the United States.

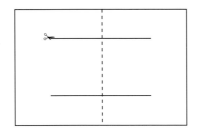

step 2

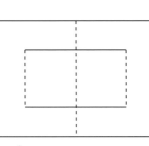

step 3

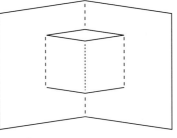

step 5

1. Start with a square. On the valley fold measure a 2" square, exactly at the center.

2. Cut along the top and bottom lines.

3. Score the side lines with a bone folder.

Left: *They Ran Out*, 1991, letterpress, linoleum cuts, pop-up with accordions that are held together by a sewn line at the fore edge, connecting the last page of one accordion with the first page of the next, 5 x 7"

Right: *They Ran Out*, partial interior

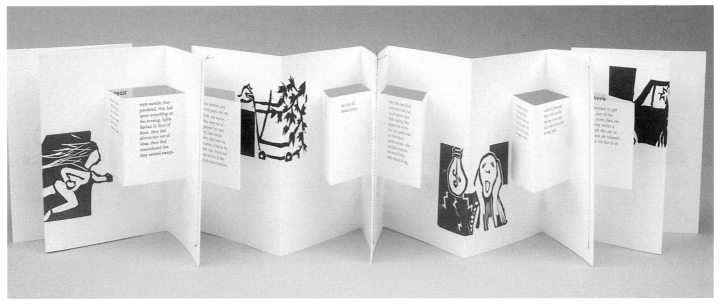

They Ran Out, complete interior

4. Fold the sides up to make valley folds.
5. Fold the original valley into a peak.

Variation #1: Fold another paper the same size and glue it to the side edges of the first, as a cover.
Variation #2: Use paper 8½ x 11". Fold in half, widthwise. Fold this folded page in half, widthwise. Unfold. Place paper in portrait orientation. Cut your pop-up image on the lower two sections with the valley fold in the middle. Fold again after your pop-up is complete for a self-contained card with a cover.
Tips: Circles must have flat sides. The center of the image can be cut the same way and folded back into a valley fold for an extra three-dimensional effect.

Uses: holiday cards, book about movement

On a Thanksgiving trip to Boston, I took books to show Ruth Rogers and Marilyn A. Hatch, librarians at Wellesley College. Marilyn also teaches the Books Arts Lab in a large print shop housed in the Margaret Clapp Library. She gave me a tour. Outside the print shop were glass cases with artists' books in them. One looked familiar. It was my book *They Ran Out*, completely open. Underneath it was a book that looked eerily similar. A student had made it. It had beautiful ink paintings on the pop-ups instead of the text. Marilyn said the student Jae-Yun Cha had patterned her book, *The Gift*, after mine for her entrance portfolio for the Yale University School of Architecture in 1991. I was flattered. She included all the details and even let the stitching "run out" at the end. *They Ran Out* has a circle of silk ivy to keep it closed. You can never run out of ivy.

Fan Book

Time: 15 minutes

Materials: a stack or set of cards or pages on cardstock approximately 1/4"
up to 2" thick, a screw post the same height as the stack of pages (hardware
stores often have aluminum screw posts; bookbinding supply stores may
have aluminum, plastic, or brass), hole punch, pencil

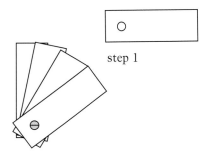

step 1

1. Punch a hole in one of your cards. Use this for a template.
2. Line up the template with the top of the next card; draw a small, light
circle in pencil on the second card.
3. Punch with the hole punch.
4. Continue until all cards are done, using the first card as the model.
5. Undo the screw post. Slide the cards onto it, then replace the top.

step 5

Uses: Guest book (each person signs one card), list poems, pocket photo
album

Variation #1: Make hard covers covered with paper or fabric (see "Hard
Covers: Covering Separate Boards," in Chapter 7, page 112.).
Variation #2: If you don't like the metallic look of the screw post, make
a circle of soft, light-weight paper or fabric, apply glue to the back, and
cover the front of the screw post, pressing the glued paper or fabric into
the groove.

Fan from offcuts of the book *Tidal Poems* (with Anne Schwartzburg), 1995, ink,
watercolor, 1 x 5 x 7/8"

Slot and Tab Book

Time: 15–30 minutes

My husband, Michael, a software engineer, designed this structure in 1995 because, he said, "glue is messy and I don't like to sew."

When he said he was going to make up a binding, I snapped, "Maybe you should learn some first!" I got to eat my words. The slot and tab is cool. My students like it. It is thick, has an exposed binding, and looks as if it has signatures.

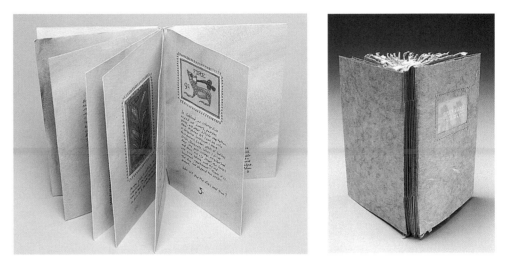

Left: *Lingering at the Window—Colors of California*, 1995, acrylics, gesso, watercolor pencil, technical pen, 4³/₄ x 7"
Right: *Waking Snakes*, 1996, letterpress, linoleum cuts on paper custom made by Magnolia Editions, slot and tab binding, 3¹/₂ x 5" book (photo by Sibila Savage)

The slot and tab structure is very similar to one that New York book artist Ed Hutchins showed me in 1994. His book had diamond-shaped cutouts for the long slits and triangles at each edge for the tabs. Three of the triangular sheets fit into three of the diamond sheets all at once. It did not create signatures, and the structure was limited by the thickness of the paper.

In 1996, Ed showed me a structure with interlocking pages. It was essentially the slot and tab, but had an extra third sheet. He had developed it independently. He said Susan Share had sent him some diagrams for a similar form.

On the diagrams I read, "These are the original drawings of that structure circa 1979–80? John Wood, retired professor (printmaking and photography) at College of Ceramics at Alfred, N.Y." Two pages fit together, but I saw that he had not linked pairs of signatures to make a thick book. I designed a cover and used the slot and tab for my edition of *Waking Snakes* in 1996.

Bookbinding is a craft in which many people share ideas and many people independently devise similar solutions to problems. If you think of something new, share it with a friend.

Materials: photocopy paper that you can cut in half; one sheet of other light-weight cover paper; knife; cutting mat; metal ruler; bone folder

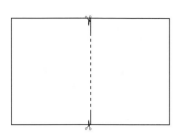

step 2

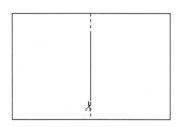

step 3

1. Photocopy paper is grained long, so cut these pages in half to make any number of sheets, $5^1/2$ x $8^1/2$", so the grain will run parallel to the spine. Then fold all cut sheets in half.

2. Cut tabs in half these pages in the following manner: along the middle fold, measure 1" from top and bottom, subtract $1/32$" and mark or cut directly. These are the tabbed sheets.

3. Cut and slot the remaining sheets by measuring 1" from top and bottom and cutting exactly from the 1" mark to 1" from the bottom (in this case, from the 1" mark to the $4^1/2$" mark). These are the slotted sheets.

4. Take one tabbed sheet, and loosely and gently roll one side of a page from top to bottom. Insert the tab through the slotted sheet, pull gently to straighten. Find the side of this "signature" that has the slotted sheet; keep it on top. You will be adding more signatures here.

5. Make pairs of pages (signatures) with the remainder of the sheets; leave these in front of you with the slotted side up. Take one signature and roll the back, tabbed sheet gently from top to bottom, inserting just as you did for the signatures, this time from the outside (keeping the slotted page closed). Add the remaining signatures in the same way, building upward. You may need to keep arranging and creasing the spine with a bone folder.

Theoretically, this structure is expandable and can be any thickness, including any number of pages. At a certain point (around 2"), however, too many pages cause the spine to wobble.

Variation: For pages with some diagonal pockets: Using an $8^1/2$ x 11" sheet, fold in half the long way, then open and fold the short way. Open. With your knife or scissors, cut a line from the fold at the bottom of the page to

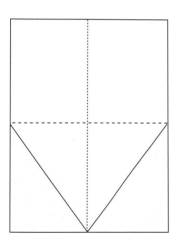

variation

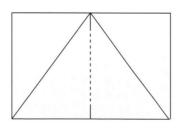

the fold at the middle side of the page. Repeat for the other side. Your paper should look as if it has a triangle at the bottom. Fold up the triangle. Tab the top and bottom; do not slit. For straight-across pockets, fold as above; trim the bottom half of your sheet at least 1" but probably no more than 2" from the middle fold. Fold up and tab.

Cover: Use other paper, preferably the same weight as the text paper, cut to $5^1/2$ x 12" (it could be as short as $10^1/2$"), grained short. Measure $4^1/4$" from one end; mark and score parallel to the grain. This section of the paper will

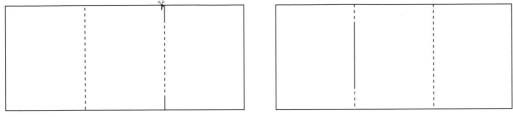

front cover   back cover

function as an interior page. Measure $4^3/8"$ from this score, and mark and score. This section will function as the cover. The remaining bit is a flap that will wrap around the first sheet when the book is fully assembled.

For best results, use a light-weight text paper, grained short or preferably with no grain. Handmade paper works particularly well.

Tip: If you use a heavy printmaking or drawing paper, such as an Arches, Rives BFK, Stonehenge, etc., you will have to cut narrow triangles instead of the tabs and diamond holes instead of the long slits.

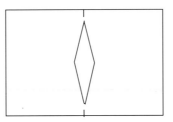

tip: diamond holes   tip: triangles

Slot and tab pieces, 1997, acrylics

Slot and tab model, 1997, acrylics, 5 x 7"

Simple Sewn Structures

learned the pamphlet stitch from Kitty Maryatt in a calligraphy class at Santa Monica High School, and I was thrilled to be able to put together a book without staples. Occasionally I take the staples out of especially nice poetry chapbooks (usually pamphlets with one set of gathered pages) and sew them back together with the pamphlet stitch.

The side-bindings were my second-favorite structure because I could easily put my pages in order. It took many years before I felt comfortable making any other kinds of books. I now know I didn't have the right tools.

Needle and Thread

Binding around dried flowers, 1997, blank book, stick binding

While any sewing needle will suffice, bookbinding needles usually have a sharp end to aid in poking holes, and a small strong eye which will not bend or collapse from the heat of your fingers. Fabric stores often carry a multi-package of several types of needles, and it may include a bookbinding needle as well as the curved needle needed for the chain stitch. Otherwise, a bookbinding supply or specialized art store may be able to sell you just one needle. They come in different sizes. If you choose ribbon for a side-bound book (ledger, stab, stick), you will likely need an embroidery needle with a larger eye. Get a few; they tend to break.

The size of needle may be determined by the type of thread you are likely to need. I generally use a medium-weight linen thread, also available at bookbinding supply stores. In the past I have successfully used a heavy-duty poly-wrapped cotton (like buttonhole thread) with a regular needle. ***In all cases, the thread should not break or stretch under stress.***

Wax your thread with beeswax to help keep it from tangling and to hold the final knot. Waxed macramé/basketmaking thread comes in many brilliant colors. It is useful and decorative for certain structures where the binding is exposed, such as stab-bindings, binding around a stick, and the chain stitch, but is generally too thick for most other bindings. If you don't buy prewaxed thread, you can purchase a small cake of beeswax at a craft or bookbinding supply store. Wax only the amount of thread you will need at one sewing by pressing the end of the thread into the beeswax, leaving 1/8" at the edge so you can grab it; put one finger on the thread to hold it down while you pull the thread and draw it across the wax. The friction will warm the wax and coat the thread.

Punching Holes

When punching holes for the stab-bindings (ledger, stick, side-bound), you may use an awl, ice pick, or bodkin (needle tool or clay tool). Always place extra cardboard under your book so you do not damage the furniture. You may also wish to use a rotating leather punch (these often have several hole sizes to choose from). These actually remove the punched material from the hole and don't leave the bunched-up paper at the back of your book. Strong hands are necessary to use this hole punch. Other people I know use a drill with a tiny bit—handheld on slow speed only! A clamp or vise would be advisable when using a drill.

For the stab-bindings, the holes need to be big enough to accommodate two or three widths of whatever thread you have chosen, because you will be sewing through them at least twice.

Clamp

A medium or large binder clip is useful to hold the pages in place while you poke holes or sew. Fold up a piece of clean paper, roughly 5 x 3", into a small pad first (probably three folds, which make it into eighths). Wrap the pad over the top of the book (four thicknesses on each side). Clamp pages with the binder clip on top of the folded paper so the clip will not directly touch or dent your book.

Knots for Simple Sewn Structures

For this section you will need to know how to make an overhand knot and a square knot.

Overhand Knot

1. Hold both ends of the string in one palm.
2. Wrap over all your fingers and across the piece in your palm.
3. Slip your fingers out and put the ends through the loop.

For smaller thread, wrap around one or two fingers only.

Square Knot

If you pull this knot very tightly, it should not come undone. If it does, either the string is too slippery or you have made a "granny knot" instead. From childhood, I still hear the chant, "Right over left, left over right."

1. Hold one end in your right hand, the other in your left.
2. Take the right piece over the left piece and back under the left piece as well.
3. Now the piece that was originally on your right is in your left hand.
4. Take this (now left) piece over the right piece (formerly the left piece) and back under the right piece.
5. Tighten.

Measuring for an Odd Number of Holes

Even without a ruler you can figure out where to punch the holes. You need a strip of paper exactly the length of the spine, from head to tail (without any hard covers).

1. Fold the paper in half, widthwise, to make it shorter and fatter. Open.
2. For three equidistant holes: from each edge, fold down to the middle. Open. Poke holes at the folds.
3. For five holes, or for less space from the edges: do step #1 then fold down the top edge between 1/2–1".
4. Fold at the middle fold, closing the paper up again.
5. Fold back the protruding edge until it is even with the other folded edge. Open.
6. Take the new fold to the middle fold, aligning it and creasing it.
7. Repeat with the opposite fold.

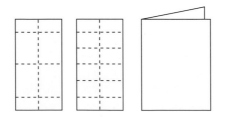

Ledger, a Hanging Book

Time: 10–20 minutes

I learned this from a Japanese bookbinding book. It looks particularly nice with different colors of raffia and with handmade clay beads. I like to think of it as a vertical-hanging book that could be kept on the wall rather than on a bookshelf. The vertical orientation makes it perfect for poetry that has short line-lengths.

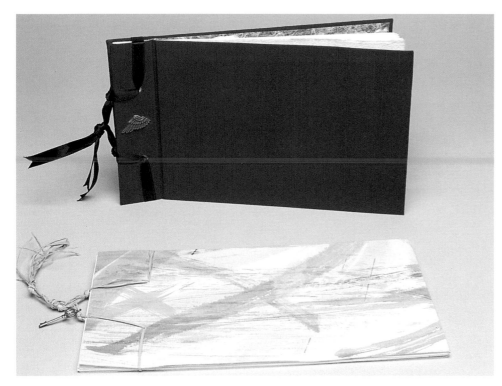

Photo album with wing, painted journal, 1995, ledger-style blank books, 9¹/₄ x 5³/₈"

Judith Tannenbaum, poet-in-residence at MacGregor Primary School, invited me to teach a book structure to second-graders in Albany, California. As people have done throughout history, I used material available; I looked in the school's supply closet and found manila covers, white drawing paper, and fat, colorful yarn for threading the book. Since the yarn could not be threaded through a needle, we wrapped the sewing end with tape so it could pass through the holes easily. The children's abilities varied; some could braid the yarn, others couldn't make an overhand knot.

Materials: stack of paper, binder clip, awl or punch, raffia or thread, wooden beads, needle, ruler, pencil, scissors

1. Stack the pages evenly, with covers top and bottom.
2. Measure 1" from the left side, 1¹/₂" from top and bottom (or pick two even places to punch holes). Mark these two places.
3. Secure at the top edge (away from the holes) with the binder clip.
4. Punch holes with the awl or leather punch.
5. Cut two pieces of raffia, each about 10" long.
6. Thread one piece through one hole, starting either at the back or front.
7. Take the same piece around the top of the book.
8. Go back through the same hole.
9. Tie at the left edge in an overhand knot.
10. Repeat with the second piece of raffia, taking it in the other hole, around the bottom edge, and back through the same bottom hole. Tie.
11. Tie the two ends (actually four strands) together with an overhand knot.

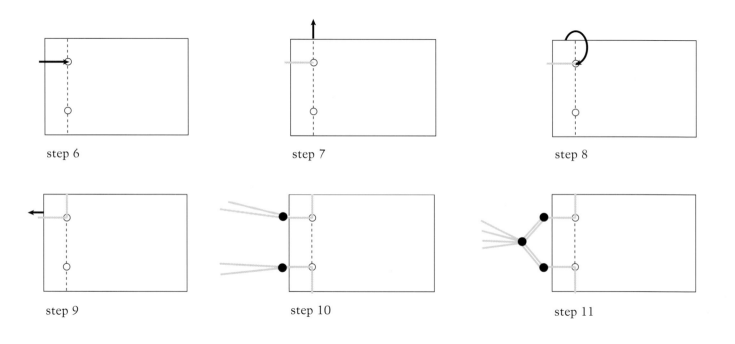

step 6   step 7   step 8

step 9   step 10   step 11

Variation #1: Run beads through the joined threads before tying.
Variation #2: Macramé the ends or braid them together.
Variation #3: Paint the covers.
Variation #4: Use papers twice as long and fold them in half, sewing the open edges together.
Variation #5: Fray the raffia ends by separating the strands and pulling them apart with your thumbnail to create a fringe.

Uses: vertical wall hanging, photo album, journal, poetry book

Stick Binding

Time: 10–15 minutes

I used a form of this binding around a plastic tube for *Taking a Look Along.* I saw the more common way of binding with a stick in *Cover to Cover,* by Shereen LaPlantz. One student in my Creative Book Structures class put the knot in the front. Then she split the raffia ends into so many strands that the book looked as if it had a hula skirt.

Left: Stick binding, 1997, acrylic ink, dyed raffia, camphor stick, blank book, 5^1/$_2$ x 4^1/$_4$"
Right: *Taking a Look Along,* 1986, letterpress, photoengravings, stick binding/single signature around tube, 4^1/$_4$ x 5^5/$_8$"

Materials: stack of paper, binder clip, awl or punch, raffia, bamboo skewer, stick, rod (etc.), pencil, ruler, scissors

1. Stack the pages evenly, including the top and bottom covers.
2. Measure one inch from the left side, one mark exactly centered and two more marks 1^1/$_2$" from the top and bottom (or just pick three places to punch holes). You can also make a jig to make even marks. See the instructions for measuring for an odd number of holes, page 42. Mark these three places.
3. Secure at the top edge (away from the holes) with the binder clip.
4. Punch holes with the awl or leather punch.

5. Cut one piece of raffia, double the width of your book (parallel to the spine).

6. Begin sewing from the back; position the stick so it bisects the holes. (You may want to glue the stick down with PVA first, to hold it.)

7. Come out the front and take the stitch over the stick and back into the same hole.

8. Proceed to the second hole from the back.

9. Go out the front, sew over the stick, and go back into the same second hole.

10. Sew from back to front through the third hole. Wrap over the stick and go back in the third hole from front to back.

11. Tie off in a square knot at the back.

Variation #1: Wind the raffia around the stick before sewing back into the holes.

Variation #2: Add more pieces of different-colored string.

Variation #3: Use dried flowers with strong stems instead of a stick.

Variation #4: For the covers, use paper twice as long, folded, with open edges at the spine. For a frame, cut a window in the front piece, and glue a picture to the exposed piece the same size as the cutout.

Variation #5: To secure a stick on a larger book, punch more holes. Sew in a similar manner, repeating the middle steps as needed.

Uses: Valentine book, nature journal, herbarium (pressed or dried leaf collection)

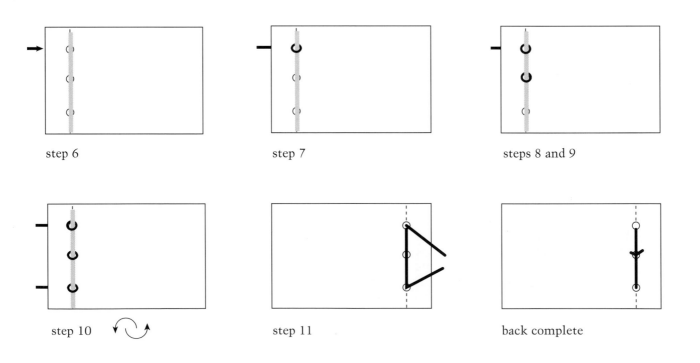

step 6   step 7   steps 8 and 9

step 10   step 11   back complete

Side-Bound Book
(stab or blockbook binding)

Time: 10–25 minutes

This structure is called the blockbook binding because it was created to hold together a series of woodblock prints long before movable type was invented. When you choose the paper, note that side-bound books are easiest to open if the pages are long and thin (in a horizontal, or landscape, format), so consider making the width of your book at least two times the height of the spine.

Materials: stack of paper, scissors, ruler, binder clip, needle, thread or ribbon, awl or leather punch, bone folder

Example: $8^1/_2$ x $5^1/_2$" (sewn along the short side)

This traditional binding works with two or more holes. To calculate thread, count out the same number of lengths (a length is the height of the book's spine from head to tail) as the number of holes plus one.

Note: In order not to become confused while sewing this book, look only at the front cover.

For two holes:
1. Pile the pages into a stack. Assemble the covers on the front and back.
2. Measure for $1^1/_2$" from the top and bottom, and one half inch from the left edge. Mark these places.

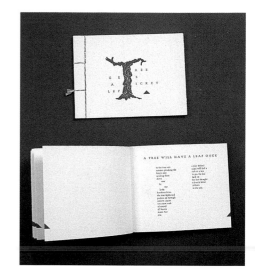

Tree Gets a Ticket Left, 1987, letterpress, side-bound, 8 x 6"

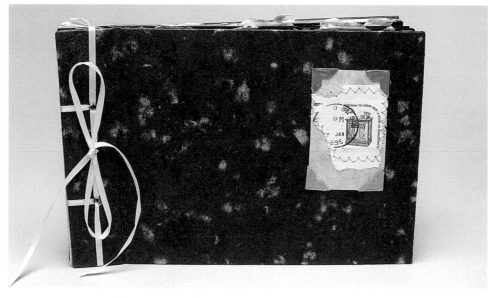

A Message, 1995, rubber stamps and postage stamps, side-bound, $7^1/_4$ x 5"

3. Poke holes with the awl.

4. For a book with two holes, take a length of thread roughly three times the width, or sewing side, of your book.

5. Start sewing by picking one hole and coming up from the back to the front, leaving a tail of thread about 3–4" long. *Do not knot.*

6. Bring the thread over the end of the book and go through the same hole again.

7. Wrap the thread over the side edge of the book and back through the same hole a third time.

8. Sew to the last hole.

9. Bring the thread over the side of the book and back through the last hole.

10. Bring the thread over the end of the book, and go back through same second (last) hole.

11. Tie off tightly in a square knot at the back of the book, centering the knot over the hole.

12. Push the knot into the hole with a bone folder if you wish.

13. Trim the ends from ¹/₈ to ¹/₂" from the knot.

For a book with three holes: Take a length of thread roughly four times the width, or sewing side, of your book. After step #7, sew into the middle hole, then bring the thread over the side of the book and back into the middle hole. Continue to the last hole (see steps #8–13).

Variation #1: Use heavy paper 1" longer than the above example. Score and fold an inch from the left margin. These folded "tabs" become spacers for a scrapbook or photo album. Sew as for side-bound book, stick, or ledger.

Variation #2: Use a lightweight Asian paper 5¹/₂ x 17". Fold in half, widthwise. With the open ends on the left and the folded edge at the fore-edge, sew these "doubled" pages.

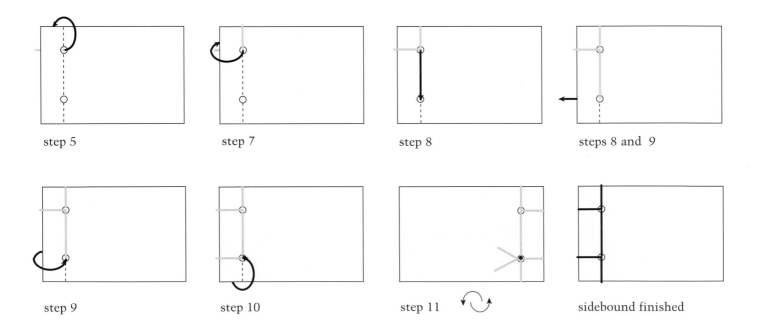

step 5   step 7   step 8   steps 8 and 9

step 9   step 10   step 11   sidebound finished

Single Signature Binding
(folding and sewing)

Time: 10–15 minutes

Materials: paper, ruler, pencil, scissors, bone folder, papers, needle, thread, binder clip, knife, cutting mat

At a Berkeley homeless shelter I asked if anyone wanted to learn a simple pamphlet stitch. Three younger men who were attending this free class said they did. We had about 45 more minutes to fill. "Would you like to do another book, with sewing?" I asked a middle-aged woman.

"Honey," she said, "I've done so much sewing in my life I don't need to do any more." The stitch is so easy, she would have been a natural at it. After I showed them that the thread wasn't doubled and taught them how to tie a square knot, the men all did fine with the sewing.

"Skip the middle" is a way to remember this sewing pattern.

For a single signature book use only enough paper, so the book will lie flat and not pop open when sewn together. For heavy paper, sew only two sheets together. With light-weight paper use approximately three to eight sheets. With many sheets you may wish to trim the fore edges with a knife, after binding. When paper cut all the same size is folded and nested, the thickness of the paper causes each successive sheet to protrude slightly. If you don't like this uneven look, trim these front edges very carefully with a utility knife.

Pencil Turns, 1991, letterpress, linoleum cuts, single signature, 4³/4 x 7"

Left: *Onion (ONe I've knOwN)*, 1994, letterpress edition, photoengravings, single signature, 6 x 8"
Right: *Onion (ONe I've knOwN)*, 1994, collage, unique book, single signature, 3³/4 x 3⁵/8" (photo by Sibila Savage)

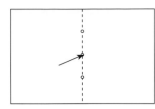

step 5

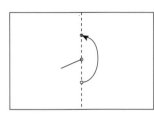

step 7

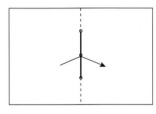

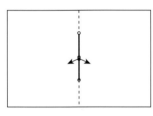

step 8

Cut only against a metal ruler. Don't try this freehand. The only problem with trimming by hand is that you risk making a ragged cut, which will mean you have to repeat the procedure and cut off more paper. Do this too many times and your book will end up much narrower than you intended. Use a very new, sharp blade for trimming and don't try to cut too thick a stack of paper.

If the book will have a hard cover or you wish to see the ends (to decorate or put beads on, etc.), start sewing from the outside. If you intend to start sewing from the inside (the knot will be inside) and you do not wish the stitching to interfere with the text or images, choose a thread the same color as your pages.

For a small pamphlet, or to add signatures to an accordion-based structure:
1. Fold the papers in half.
2. Nest the pages inside each other.
3. With the binder clip, clamp half the book at the top or bottom.
4. Poke three holes in the fold, at even intervals, leaving at least one half inch from each end.

Sewing pattern:
5. Start with the middle hole.
6. Go back out to one end hole.
7. Skip the middle and make a long stitch to the other end hole.
8. Come back through the middle, and tie a square knot around the long stitch. It should look like two stitches now.

Sewing pattern for a larger book:
Use five holes. If the book is really enormous, a larger, odd number of holes is fine. Start at the middle hole, as for the pamphlet. Instead of making the long stitch immediately, sew a running stitch up to the head of the book and back down toward the middle again. When you get to the hole immediately neighboring the middle hole, skip the middle and proceed the same way, tying off in a square knot.

Variation: Cut the pages into different shapes before you sew (i.e., graduated sections of an onion) or when the sewing is complete (i.e., the slanted top of a tea bag).

Uses: program, wedding booklet, poetry book, short story

Teachings of Sourgrass, 1995, from *A Garden Variety Book*, Book Two, letterpress, mixed media, seed-packet slipcase, single signature, 3^{1}/2 x 5^{1}/2"

Two-Sewn-as-One

Time: 15–20 minutes

When Mollie was seven months old, I decided she was like a magpie, because she liked to pick up bits of shiny things, and like a mockingbird, because she could imitate sounds. For the book about her, I used the two-sewn-as-one and tabbed the inner pages to differentiate between magpie and mockingbird. I gave copies of the book to all our relatives.

The two-sewn-as-one is the easiest way to make a thicker, more "booklike" book. You don't need any special skills or lots of practice. I learned this book from Betsy Davids in art school.

Materials: Eight sheets of paper $5^1/2$ x $8^1/2$", folded in half; thread, needle, binder clip, awl, cardboard to protect table

1. Fold the papers in half to make pages $5^1/2$ x $4^1/4$".
2. Make two sets or signatures of papers, nesting four sheets, one inside the other for each, with back folds aligned.
3. Keeping their folds back-to-back and still nested, open the two signatures and clip them with a binder clip to hold.
4. Poke the desired odd number of holes.
5. Sew as for a single signature.
6. When done, fold up again into the two signatures back-to-back; then fold these together, one atop the other, and smooth them down with the bone folder.

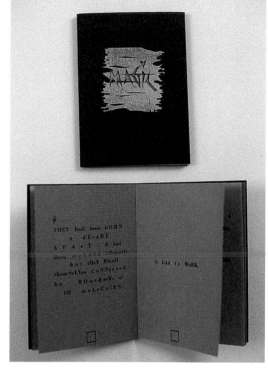

Magic, 1988, letterpress edition, engravings, two-sewn-as-one, $3^3/4$ x $5^1/4$"

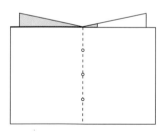

step 4, with soft cover

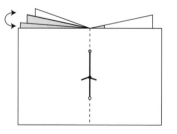

steps 5 and 6, with soft cover

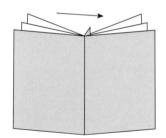

step 6, with soft cover

finished, with soft cover

For best results, press them flat between two Masonite boards held down with bricks or under heavy books.

Variation #1: For a soft cover: before sewing cut a cover sheet twice the width of the book plus one or two inches. Fold the cover in half. Fold back the one or two inches to make a tiny M-shaped accordion in the middle. Tuck this tab between the two signatures before sewing, with one signature in each of the valleys.

Left: *Magpie and Mockingbird*, 1992, letterpress, linoleum cuts, two-sewn-as-one, 5¹/₄ x 8¹/₄"
Right: *She Said I Like Almost Anything from a Distance*, 1987, letterpress, linoleum cuts, two-sewn-as-one, 6 x 8"
(photo by Saul Schumsky)

Variation #2: Use same method as above, except use decorative paper facing the signatures, and glue the backs to a hard cover.
Variation #3: Make the tab the same width as the signature pages.
Variations #4 and 5: Make a soft-wrap cover or make a wrapped hard cover.

Uses: collaborative book with two different points of view opening from both sides, simple hardcover journal, guest book

Tea Bag Book
Folding tea bag-like pages (folding and cutting)

I had made a series of prints and put them together in a portfolio, all called *A Tea Party*. When I approached a local gallery in Berkeley to see if they would show the portfolio, they were hesitant about just showing prints. I suggested a tea show. For the show I figured out how to fold a tea bag and started making collages with the tea bags and old stamps. My sister, Nina, wanted a collage. She framed it in a shadowbox and put the collage in her kitchen. Her friends saw it and wanted it. I made more.

Materials: paper, knife and cutting mat, pencil, binder clip, bone folder, awl or leather punch, metal-edged ruler, needle, embroidery or other thread

Use a thin paper (i.e. mulberry, silk tissue, glassine) that is double the length of your finished book plus double your "fold-in" tea bag base. (A 4 x 6" finished book would have 9 x 6" papers folded in half with 1/2" folded in on each side of the middle, for example.)

For covers use heavier paper (such as Canson Mi Teintes), folded in half only. (In the above example, the cover papers would be 8 x 6", folded in half, grained short.)

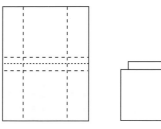

steps 1, 2, 3   step 3

1. Fold six papers in half. Open them.
2. Score a 1/2–1" line on each side of the fold. Close again.
3. Fold it back on itself (at score marks) like an accordion. Do both sides in this manner.
4. Repeat for all six sheets.
5. Measure 1/2" down and 1/2" across. Mark.
6. Line up the ruler with the two diagonal marks, and trim off the corners.
7. Line up the pages with the open end to your left and the folded edge to your right. Clip them together with the binder clip over a few folded-up pieces of scrap paper so the clip is not directly touching your book.
8. Proceed with one of the stab-bindings.

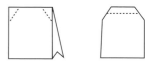

single tea bag

To make a single tea bag: Do steps 1, 2, and 3, fold the corners in, fold the top over, and last, staple a 5" piece of embroidery thread or string to the tea bag. Attach the tag as described on page 54.

single tea bag complete

For Tea Bag Shape on Single Signature Book

For the tea exhibit, I also made the little tea bag-shaped book *Mrs. White Has Tea*. It is about colors and friendship. I dedicated it to Mollie, who at age two asked me to read it over and over.

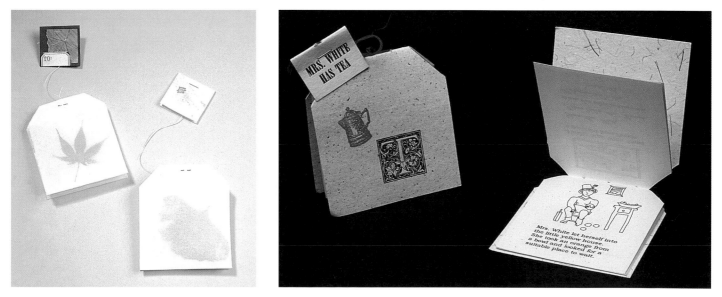

Left: Tea Bag Cards, 1997, glassine, Japanese maple leaf, ginkgo, rubber stamps, 3 x 3 1/2"
Right: *Mrs. White Has Tea*, 1993, photocopy, letterpress and rubber stamp cover, single signature, 3 x 3 1/4"

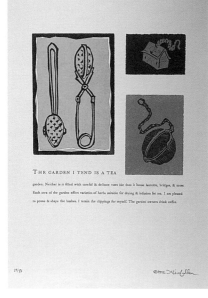

The Garden I Tend, 1995, letterpress and linoleum cuts on paper from *A Tea Party* portfolio of prints, 11 x 15"

First, make a single-signature book, sewing from the outside and leaving one 5" tail to attach to the tag. Trim the other thread.

1. Measure evenly from the corner along the edge on the folded side, top and bottom.
2. Using a metal-edged ruler and knife, cut off the corners.

Variation: Make pages in other shapes such as hearts, or the graduated ovals as in the one-of-a-kind book *Onion* (photo on page 49).

Making a Tag

Make a tag with a rectangle of medium-weight paper folded in half.

1. Thread the needle through the 5" tail of thread.
2. Go in the folded rectangle and out again and back in again, creating one stitch.
3. Tie off the thread to itself. Trim.
4. Staple closed at the edge.

For a hard tag: cut a square of 4-ply museum board into a square, approximately 2". Punch a hole in the board with a leather punch or hole punch, awl, eyelet punch, etc. Tie the ends of the thread to the hole.

Uses: invitation or party favor for a tea party

Simple Adhesive Structures

 With small amounts of thinly spread glue you can quickly connect many pages to make notepad-like books, a flower structure, accordion-folded books, and scrolls.

Use a small brush or strip of board to apply polyvinyl acetate when making the books in this chapter. Work atop layers of clean scrap paper (old magazines) so you can discard any sticky sheets.

A Note on Glue

You can make most of the simple adhesive structures in this chapter with PVA. Polyvinyl Acetate or Adhesive (PVA) is a white synthetic glue that dries quickly and remains flexible and strong. PVA dries clear but shiny and will show, especially if it gets on book cloth.

Wheat paste is an organic substance that dries more slowly and allows a little time for repositioning if necessary. Paste is easier to wipe off book cloth. I often like to use a combination of both to obtain the advantages of each. The projects described may require paste or glue or a combination.

If your paste or glue is too thick, add only **distilled water** to thin it. Distilled water is most important if you are using all archival materials and wish to keep the book acid-free. Otherwise, the acids in the tap water may eventually cause spots to appear on your book.

A good glue brush needn't be expensive. I like using round, flat-bottomed stencil brushes in a medium to large size (1–2" diameter). The glue can be applied evenly and the short bristles make it easy to clean. Wash brushes right away when finished. Make sure you have rinsed out all the adhesive. When dry, PVA is extraordinarily difficult to get out of brushes, but you can soak it out with warm water over a few days.

When working with children or making a mock-up or sample, you may wish to use a glue stick. In general, the adhesive in a glue stick is not as strong and the book may fall apart. Pritt glue stick is the stickiest and is pH neutral, but takes a long time to dry (which can be good if you want to reposition something). It can be difficult to locate; however, it is available through some mail-order sources of archival materials. Scotch permanent adhesive glue stick, sold by mail order companies, is also pH neutral and archival.

In all cases, when working with adhesives, place waxed paper between pages that have been glued together, and press the book under a heavy book or under boards and weights overnight.

Wheat Paste Recipes

Cooked Wheat Paste (for approximately four cups of paste)
1 cup or one part flour (you may use food-grade flour if necessary)

4 cups or four parts distilled water (you may use clean or filtered tap water)

Cook over medium-high heat, stirring constantly with a wire whisk until the mixture thickens. Cook five minutes or more after it thickens (longer cooking is said to produce better paste). Cover and cool, placing the saucepan in a container of cool water. Refrigerate tightly covered. The paste keeps for several days, at most a week or two. Strain if necessary. The paste can also be made in the top of a double boiler over hot water or in a microwave. If you use a microwave, you will need to look at it and stir every 30 seconds to prevent it from bubbling over and getting lumpy.

Based on a recipe from *Japanese Bookbinding* by Kojiro Ikegami

For Paste That Is Not Cooked
Daniel Smith, Inc., in Seattle, Washington, sells wheat paste powder that does not require cooking. While you can buy wheat paste from art supply stores, I prefer this archival wheat paste powder. I have tried various wheat starch pastes, but find them too gelatinous, hard to spread, and hard to mix with PVA. I now stay away from packages with the word "starch" on the label. If the archival quality of the paste is not crucial to you, use wallpaper paste or flour-type thickeners.

To mix paste and water or paste and glue: Add small amounts of the dry powder paste directly to glue or water and stir quickly. It works like oatmeal: when it sits it gets thicker, so give it a minute or so before you add more paste; preferably, mix the batch half an hour before you begin to work. If the paste gets too thick, add water (use distilled water to keep the adhesive acid-free), tiny amounts at a time to prevent it from getting lumpy. If it does become hopelessly lumpy, strain the paste with a kitchen strainer that you use only for this purpose. Straining works faster when the paste is thinner. Check the consistency; add more paste if you need to. The thickness of paste needed depends on the project; usually, it should be somewhere between oozing and firm when it stands on a plate.

A batch of glue/paste will keep, tightly sealed, in the refrigerator about two weeks, if you pour a little at a time into another container, such as a paper plate, and dip your brush into that container instead of your main batch. Hairs, fibers, and other material contaminate the adhesive and encourage mold to grow, even in full-strength PVA glue.

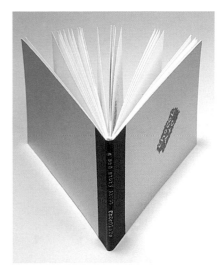

A Sad Story About Chocolate, 1989, photocopy, linoleum cut, rubber stamps, perfect-bound, 5¹/₂ x 4¹/₄"

Perfect Binding
(gluing)

Time: 5–10 minutes

Betsy Davids showed me how to do this in college. I was astonished to find I could bind the whole edition of 100 copies of *A Sad Story About Chocolate* in five minutes. You can re-glue mass-market paperbacks that are coming apart with this method. Prepare the book block, then attach the cover at the spine.

Materials: stack of pages, PVA glue, glue brush, weight, binder clip (for small stack only) or clamp

Optional: strip of paper for additional spine, ruler, bone folder, pencil

This book structure works only with PVA glue. Glue many books all lined up together in one stack. Use a knife to slice them apart when dry. For notepads, you may wish to use padding compound, available in some stationery/office supply stores. The only advantage to the compound is that the pages tear off more easily.

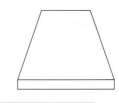

steps 1, 4, and 5

1. Line up the loose pages in a stack at the edge of a table.
2. Clip the edge with a binder clip, and clamp together or weight down using a heavy book or brick, with the stack edge unweighted slightly over the edge of the table.
3. Spread glue thickly on the spine edge. Let dry.

step 7

For a more finished appearance:
4. Cut a spine from a contrasting piece of paper the same height as your book (paper grained long) and three times the depth of the book.
5. Measure a third from each edge of the spine (or by bending the paper around the book).
6. Score the paper with a bone folder or your fingernail along the edge of a ruler.
7. Adhere the strip to the spine of the book with more PVA, hiding the previously glued piece.

complete

Uses: notepads, a postcard collection, any pile of pages to be bound quickly

step 1 finding a square

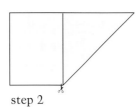

step 2

step 3

Flower fold model, 1997, Thai reversible Unryu paper, 1^{1}/$_{2}$ x 1^{1}/$_{2}$"

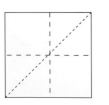

steps 2, 3, and 4

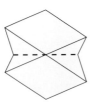

step 6

Finding a Square

If you don't have a square piece of paper, you can easily make one. Fold one corner of a rectangular paper diagonally, so the corner lines up with one side of the paper. Crease the diagonal. Cut off the excess and discard. The folded paper, when opened, is a perfect square.

Flower Fold
(folding and gluing) from colored square paper

Time: 10–15 minutes

I think a student showed me this one.

Materials: origami paper or other square paper, glue or glue stick, small brush for gluing, bone folder

1. Put the paper on a work surface, colorful side down (or place face-down the side that will be the outside).
2. Fold the paper in half. Open.
3. Fold in half the other way. Turn over.
4. Fold diagonally. Open. Turn over.
5. Put your finger down on the very center to "pop" up the corners.
6. Take the corners that have the diagonal fold through them and bring them together; while doing this, fold in the sides. You should have a square with two flat sides and folds in between.
7. Repeat these steps with four or more pieces of paper.
8. Line up the squares with their opening to the right.
9. Put glue on one of the flat sides with the opening facing to the right (it will look like a diamond shape).
10. Place another diamond on top of this one, lining it up carefully.
11. Press down.
12. Repeat for the rest of your squares.

Anna Wolf alternates right-opening squares and left-opening ones for her diamond-fold books.

Variation: Put the loose ends together. With a hole punch, punch through both pieces; then, thread a ribbon or raffia through to make a hanging decoration.

Uses: decorative star or ornament; put one descriptive word inside each "petal" and use as a greeting or friendship card; write about flowers, stars, or other things that unfold or blossom

Album/Flutterbook
(folding and gluing)

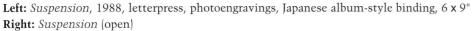

Time: 10–20 minutes

This binding is not a photo album. I call this album the Japanese album to differentiate it, because I learned it from *Japanese Bookbinding,* by Kojiro Ikegami. I used it for *Suspension*. My book is about a woman and the bureaucracy. She goes to turn herself in to the unnamed "authorities" and has to wait in line. Many times I have felt I was between things, suspended; that uneasy feeling was what I was trying to evoke. Venus is sewn "suspended" on the front cover. I printed directly from hand-inked lace.

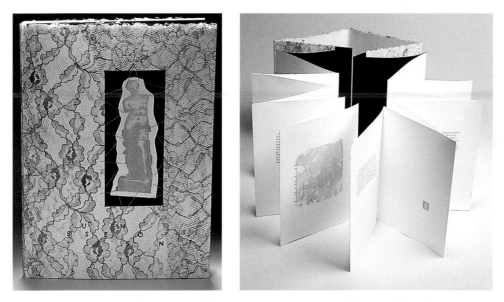

Left: *Suspension*, 1988, letterpress, photoengravings, Japanese album-style binding, 6 x 9"
Right: *Suspension* (open)

Materials: paper, glue (glue stick may not hold this completely), small brush for gluing, magazines for scrap paper, waxed paper

Example: 4^1/$_4$ x 5^1/$_2$" book from paper 5^1/$_2$ x 8^1/$_2$"

Both structures begin in the same manner. The album style has folded pages glued at the fore edge. For the flutterbook, the folded pages are glued at the spine. The waxed paper will prevent moisture from the glue from being absorbed by subsequent pages, which would warp the book.

Tips: For cleaner gluing, place a sheet of scrap paper over the sheet you wish to glue, leaving only the edge that will actually be glued. Spread the

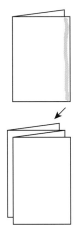

glue, remove the scrap paper, and proceed with the remaining pages. Work from the last page to the first, aligning the pages and stacking as you go. Use a minimum of glue.

1. Fold the pages in half. Face the open edges to the right.
2. Put a sheet of scrap paper inside one page.
3. Spread the glue in a thin, flat line along the fore edge of one sheet.
4. Remove the scrap paper and discard it, replacing it with a sheet of waxed paper.
3. Set another on top. Line up.
4. Do the rest of the pages this way to make the Japanese album style.

For the flutterbook: Spread glue in a thin line along the side of the spine (just to the right, not on the fold itself), stack another sheet on top, and continue in this manner with all sheets.

Variation #1: Make a soft cover or wrapped hard cover.
Variation #2: Use a series of single-sided photocopies for your pages because the printing only needs to be on one side.

Uses: travel journal, sketch book

step 3

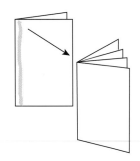

flutterbook

Concertina with Tabs
(folding and gluing)

Time: 10–15 minutes

"Arts and crafts class," someone called out. A woman and a man sat down at the table we had just covered with a plastic tablecloth. Lisa Kokin rounded up a few more uncommitted students.

"We have a guest teacher. We're making books tonight," she said. An elderly man and a middle-aged woman were roped in. Another younger man sat down at the end.

"I'll try it," he said, shrugging.

At a Berkeley homeless shelter we made the concertina with tabs using strips of magazines to attach the inner folded papers. We made thick books quickly. The students seemed pleased with the results. The men and women looked through the strips thoughtfully for images that appealed to them; they didn't just take random pieces. I made Life Stories *as an example during that class.*

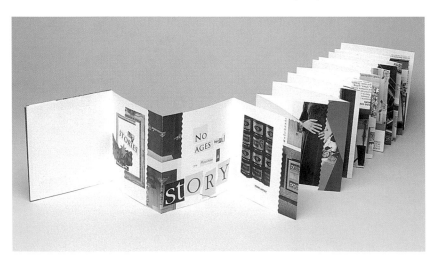

Life Stories, 1996, collage, unique book, accordion with tabs, 4^1/$_4$ x 4^3/$_4$"

Rock Dove, 1988, letterpress, linoleum cuts, photocopy, 4 x 10" (photo by Sibila Savage)

I used tabs to hold the concertinas together for the bottom part of *Rock Dove*. The Mexican bark paper was brittle, so I didn't want to poke holes and try to sew it, for fear of tearing it.

Materials: pages $5^1/2$ x $8^1/2$"; decorative tabs or strips, grained long and at least $1^1/2$" wide x $5^1/2$" tall, PVA glue or glue stick, glue brush, scrap paper, waxed paper

For a cover: Use two pieces of contrasting paper the same size as your inner pages, fold in half, and affix them in the same manner, one at the front and one at the back.

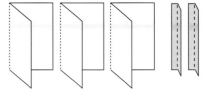

steps 1, 2, 3, 4

1. Fold all the pages in half.
2. Face the pages with the open end to the right.
3. Fold all tabs or strips in half, lengthwise.
4. Face the folded strips with the open end to the left.
5. Place the waxed paper inside one page.
6. Place one strip on a sheet of scrap paper and brush glue on the inside of the strip.
7. Line up the top sheet of one page so it is even with the fold on the strip. Rub the page down on the strip. The strip should be at the fore edge.
8. Quickly line up the bottom of another sheet, so when you close the sticky strip, two pages will be adhered into a concertina.
9. Continue gluing strips and aligning the pages: page, strip open, page, press strip closed, until done.

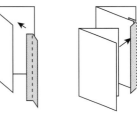

step 7   step 8

Variation: Use adhesive linen tape in place of glued strips. Hide this joint on the back of the pages instead of around the front edges.

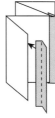

step 9

Uses: recipe book, journal, guest book

Endless Accordion
(folding and gluing)

Time: 10–20 minutes

This structure does not depend on one long piece of paper folded up precisely, but on a series of short, easy M-shaped accordion-folds. Although it appears endless, this structure works best if it is kept under 1/2" thick. The spine of this accordion starts to curve to the right if you use more than approximately ten strips.

Materials: six inner pages, 5¹/2 x 8¹/2"; five decorative tabs or strips, grained long, at least 1¹/2" wide x 5¹/2" tall; two heavier, decorative cover pages (same size as inner pages); PVA glue or glue stick; old glossy magazines for scrap paper; glue brush; bone folder

Example: 5¹/2 x 4¹/4" book (with six pages)

Make five M-shaped concertinas (accordions) by folding the strips in half, lengthwise; then fold the edges back to the middle fold. Turn them all toward you so that when tightly closed, the concertina opens from the right (like any regular book in English). Put these accordion strips on your left.

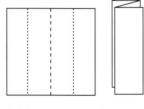

folding an accordion

To glue:
1. Open the flaps of one of the M's.
2. Using scrap paper, cover all but the edge you need to glue.
3. Brush on the glue. Remove the scrap paper.
4. Press the flap down on the top of the last page.
5. Put glue on the top flap, align, and press the second-to-last page on top of the flap.
6. Glue a second M on top of this page.
7. Continue until all M's and pages are glued together in alternating order.

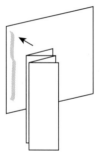

step 4

Variation #1: Glue recipe cards to the M's.
Variation #2: Use folded pages, gluing the open edges of each page together at the spine.

Uses: recipe book, photo album

I started out to create only a model of the endless accordion, but ended up with a finished piece. First, I decided to use tabbed index cards. So I glued those together with the accordions. It looked so empty. I rummaged around and found some old recipes I always thought I would make but never did. They were yellowed. I glued them to the cards. "Yeah, so what?" I said to myself. I got out the *New York Times* and found two articles, one about a beauty queen factory in Venezuela, the other about how the employees of the FDA don't eat according to their own standards. I mixed them up and glued parts of each in the book. I didn't like it. I ripped some of the recipes

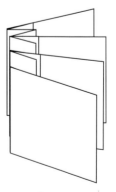

complete

off, thinking it would be funnier if each tab had the wrong title for the recipe below it. Then I thought of a text and rubber-stamped it around the torn paper. I added some decorative torn papers. *Eat As I Say: unrecognizable recipes* was born.

Eat As I Say: unrecognizable recipes, 1997, collage, rubber stamps, unique book, endless accordion, 6 x 4³/₈"

Tunnel Book
(folding, cutting, gluing)

Time: 10–45 minutes (depending on whether or not you are cutting out images)

The first tunnel book I made was *Gateway*. I saw later that just gluing pages into one long accordion-folded paper made the pictures/pages stand at a diagonal, and the tunnel didn't open completely. After examining some of Edward H. Hutchins's tunnel books, I began using this method instead. It is similar to the endless accordion, but can be thicker because it has two "spines."

The tunnel book offers a challenge to the maker: how to see many layers at once. The finished piece is dramatic.

Gateway, 1992, letterpress, torn paper, tunnel book, 5 x 7"

Materials: metal ruler, pencil, knife, cutting mat, stencil brush, small brush for gluing, at least five photocopies or original art/prints or picture postcards of the same or different 5¹/₂" (tall) image(s) (drawing, photograph, text) onto cardstock or heavy paper, grain vertical (from 6" up to 8¹/₂" wide), old magazine as scrap paper, bone folder, papers (eight pieces, 3 x 5¹/₂") grained long, for spine-flaps, glue

Example: 5¹/₂ x 6–8¹/₂" book

New Mexico, 1995, photocopy, colored pencil, tunnel book, 4¹/₄ x 5¹/₂"

Tips: Pick a horizontal/landscape drawing with perspective or with many objects in it that are clearly defined. Or pick an abstract image or series of images that you can add to by cutting out your own interesting shapes. The pictures should have at least a ¹/₂" border on the sides.

 1. Pick the image that is to be the final one. Set it aside. You will not cut this one.
 2. Cut a large hole in the first image. You can vary the shape of the holes or cut out distinct objects in each layer.

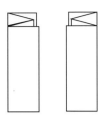

steps 5 and 6

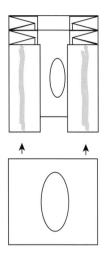

step 10

3. Cut holes of decreasing size into the other three images. The top and bottom can be cut to within ¹/₈".

4. Make eight M-shaped concertinas (accordions) by folding the strips in half, lengthwise; then, fold the edges back to the middle fold.

5. Turn one toward you so that when tightly closed, the concertina opens from the right (like a regular book in English). Put this accordion on your left.

6. Take another one that would open from the left and put it to the right of your work surface.

7. When gluing, open the flaps. Cover with scrap paper all but the end you need to glue. Brush on the glue. Remove the scrap paper. Press the flap down to the image.

8. Glue your last image (the one without any holes) to the back two flaps (one on either side). The flaps will be glued on top of the last image. Glue the pages from back to front, from the smallest hole to the largest.

9. Next, glue the fourth page on top of the flaps, then glue two more flaps on top of the fourth image.

10. Repeat with all the images. The first image should sit on top of the flaps.

Uses: birthday card, presentation book, table decoration, one poem

Accordion-Fold Book
(cutting, folding, gluing)

Time: 10–20 minutes

Accordion-fold (concertina) books make the best books for displaying under glass because the pages can be revealed simultaneously. Use any size paper, but allow for a tab of at least one half inch. I learned this accordion-fold technique from Betsy Davids.

Materials: bone folder, pencil, knife and cutting mat, glue, glue brush, scrap paper, waxed paper

Example: 5 x 5¹/₂" book, using two sheets of paper 5¹/₂ x 21"

1. Cut off an inch from one of the papers, making it 5¹/₂ x 20".

2. On the other sheet, mark, score, and fold in an inch parallel to the shorter side.

3. Keeping the tab folded, fold this sheet in half, matching one cut edge to the fold with the tab inside.

4. Fold the ends to the middle fold, one end at a time. Open and turn over. You should have valley, peak, valley, peak.

5. Fold the 20" sheet in half.

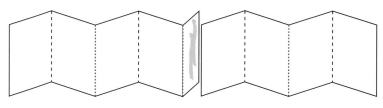

6. Fold the ends back to the new fold and crease, making sure they are aligned. Open. You should have valley, peak, valley.

7. Apply glue in a thin, flat line to the front of the tab on the sheet.

8. Set the other sheet on top. Press down. The tab will be hidden behind the second sheet.

steps 7 and 8

Variation #1: Add a wrapped hard cover with removable spine or an adhesive hard cover (no spine).

Variation #2: Put pop-ups in the valley folds first.

Uses: display of small pictures, photo album, sketch book or journal, guest or honor book

Circle Accordion
(cutting, folding, taping, or gluing)

Time: 15–25 minutes

The circle accordion is a good first book.

I taught this structure to my friend Nan Wishner, a poet and writing teacher who likes craftwork but hadn't had any previous experience making books. When I returned to her house I noticed a dozen of these books in her dining room. She said she was thrilled with the feel of the thick, squishy book and particularly liked using the linen tape. She had visited her friends Marc and Wendy and taught them this structure. Wendy kept her finished book by her plate at the dinner table and kept looking at it very proudly.

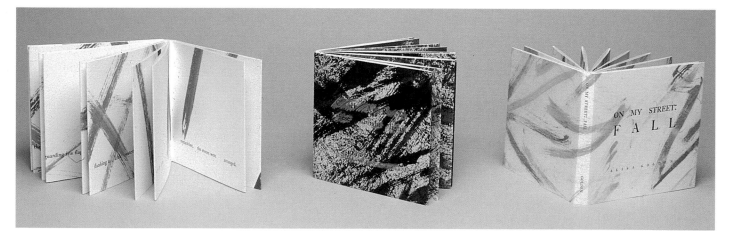

Walking on the Sentence Stones, Chart: These Bright Lights, On My Street: Fall, 1997, letterpress, acrylic inks, gesso, circle accordions, 5^1/$_2$ x 5"

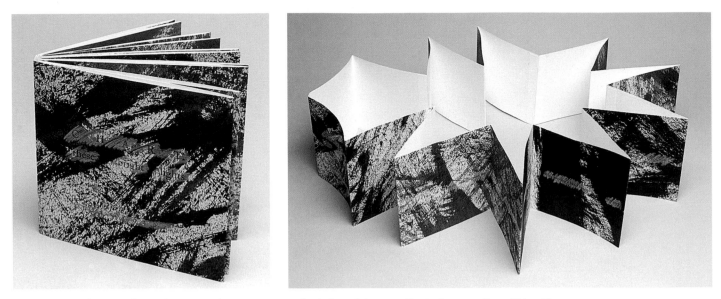

Left: *Chart: These Bright Lights*, 1997, letterpress, acrylic inks, white pencil, circle accordion, 5¹/₂ x 5"
Right: *Chart: These Bright Lights* (open)

When fully open, this accordion makes a modified circle with all the pages connected. I developed it because I was dissatisfied with accordion books that were not attached to their front covers. Other bookmakers may have done the same structure, but I don't remember seeing any quite like this.

Note: The depth of the spine may vary, depending on the thickness of the paper.

Materials: knife and cutting mat, self-adhesive archival linen tape, bone folder, pencil, metal-edged ruler

Example: A 6 x 5¼" book, using five pieces of medium-to-heavy paper, 6 x 22" long, can be cut from one 22 x 30" sheet of printmaking or drawing paper.

   1. Pick one piece of paper to be your cover. Cut off ½" to make it 6 x 21½". Measure 10½" from each edge and mark and score. You should have a ½" spine in the center.
   2. Fold each edge in to the closest center fold. You may wish to score the paper first at the 5¼-inch mark.
   3. With the remaining sheets, cut 1" off the edges, to create four sheets that are each 6 x 21".
   4. Fold one sheet in half. (If it has writing or a design on it, fold right-side-in.) Crease it well with the bone folder. You will have peak, valley, peak.
   5. Keeping the paper folded, bring the ends back to the middle fold, align, and crease well.
   6. Repeat for all four sheets.
   7. Cut five 6" lengths of linen tape.

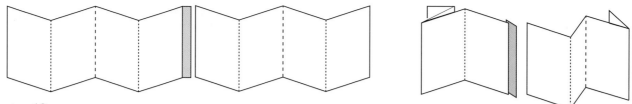

step 10

8. Start connecting the pages by placing the cover piece in front of you, the outside cover facing up.

9. Take the backing off one piece of the tape. Attach the tape to the edge of the cover, sticky-side up, leaving half the sticky side available.

10. Attach the next page by aligning it with the cover ends and pressing down on the available half of the tape.

11. Continue to tape and attach pages until you get to the last one. Tape the last page to the back flap of the cover in the same manner.

Variation: Paint the large sheet first with acrylic paints or inks before you cut it into strips.

Uses: texts that involve life cycles, seasons, or other recurring events

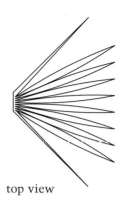

top view

Hand Scroll
(sanding, painting, gluing)

Time: 15 minutes to prepare dowels and 10–15 minutes to glue paper and ribbon

I printed a linoleum cut and several copies of the text by Morihei Ueshiba, the founder of Aikido, a defensive Japanese martial art. I bound one sheet into a hanging scroll for my Aikido instructor, Elizabeth Lynn. A second copy I made into the hand scroll *Heaven*. The scroll is a very traditional book structure in Japan.

I recommend preparing the dowels for scrolls one day and drying them overnight before continuing. Make a long, thin box to store and protect your hand scroll.

Materials: knife, cutting mat, scissors, ruler, pencil, brushes, scrap paper, flat ribbon or cord approximately 18" long, 7 x 6" decorative or contrasting cover paper, awl, one 7" piece of half-round reed, one 8" wooden dowel, sandpaper, PVA glue, hammer, two 1" brads or nails, one or two wooden drawer pulls (optional), acrylic paints

Example: 7" scroll from mulberry paper, *chiri* (with no inclusions such as bits of bark or confetti), *Yatsuo*, or other non-creasing Asian papers cut to 7 x 10–25", grained short or no grain (you may make the smaller 7 x 10" sec-

Heaven by Morihei Ueshiba, 1996–1997, letterpress, linoleum cut, acrylics and gesso, handscroll with raffia, 11" dowel, 9 x 18" mulberry paper

tions from different kinds of papers and then glue them together at the edges to make a longer piece)

1. Sand the ends of the dowel.
2. Put down layers of old magazines for scrap paper.
3. If you wish to add a small wooden drawer-pull for a knob at the end: hammer a 1" brad into the end of the dowel, put glue on the end of the dowel and inside the hole in the drawer-pull, and glue the knob to one end of the dowel. You may wish to have knobs at both ends.
4. Paint the ends with acrylic paint if desired (the middle will have paper covering it). Dry.
5. Brush about a 1" flat line of PVA glue along the left end of the long scroll paper.
6. Wrap the paper around the dowel. Smooth down.
7. On one end of the cover paper measure $1/2$" in from the 7" side. Score a line with your bone folder.
8. Glue down the half-round reed strip on the back, flat-side-up, along the score.
9. Clip very small bits of the corners diagonally.
10. Apply more glue to the back of the cover (the flap you just made) and fold it over the reed. Press down.
11. Use a bone folder to smooth and flatten the paper against the reed strip.
12. Make a line of glue on the very front edge of the text sheet of the scroll.
13. Glue down the front or outside of the cover on top of this edge, aligning it carefully. Smooth down.

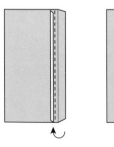

steps 5, 12, and 13

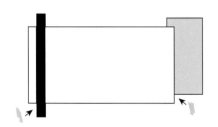

steps 8, 9, and 10

steps 10 and 11

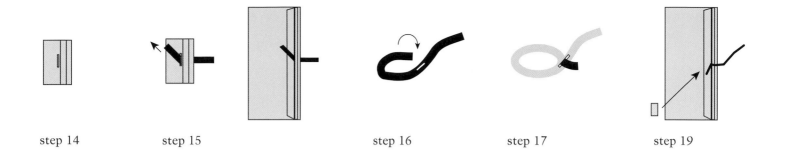

14. Cut a slit for the cord or ribbon in the cover paper, centered, just behind the reed strip.
15. Poke the cord from the right side to the inside. (For threading, it may help to wrap the end with cellophane tape.) Leave only about $1/2$" showing.
16. Make a small slit at the short end.
17. Thread the long end all the way through it.
18. Trim the short end. Glue down the inside.
19. Paste a small bit of the cover paper over it. Dry.
20. Roll up the scroll and wind the cord.

complete

Uses: birthday poem or wish, personal message or greeting, sample book of Asian papers

Variation: Omit the 7 x 16" covering paper. Use a longer text paper, and paint a section at the end with acrylics and gesso, covering both sides of the paper. The painted part will serve as a decorative cover.

Winding a Hand Scroll

According to a traditional Japanese bookbinder, the cord should wrap around the scroll $3^{1}/_{2}$ times, each turn of the cord moving down the scroll slightly, the end tucking in partway. My husband visited a shop in Japan where he learned to wind a scroll. He taught me.

To wind: Hold the scroll in the left hand and wind the cord around one or two fingers that are resting on the scroll. When you remove your fingers, you will tuck the looped end into this space. Adjust the tightness by pulling the loop and tightening at the end. Pull back and forth until the cord is snug.

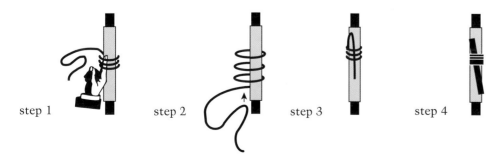

step 1　　　　　step 2　　　　　step 3　　　　　step 4

Hanging Scroll

Volume I, 1995, collagraphs, letterpress, acrylics and gesso, hanging scroll, 11" painted dowels, 7 x 21½" mulberry paper, and *Heaven*, 1996–1997

Time: 20 minutes to prepare dowels and 10–25 minutes to glue paper and ribbon

Marilyn Webberley has some nice scrolls in her how-to book *Books, Boxes and Wraps*. Another good source is *Japanese Bookbinding*, by Kojiro Ikegami. *Where We Get Our Hopes (Wishing Scroll)* is my first hanging scroll. I used gel medium to attach the objects to a woodblock. Then I coated the entire surface with three coats of the gel medium. When it dried, I inked the block and printed the "collagraph." I painted the endpapers with acrylics mixed with lots of gesso. Gesso keeps the paper from sticking when it is rolled up.

Materials: hammer, four 1" brads or nails, four wooden drawer pulls, acrylic paints, sandpaper, ribbons, one long "text" paper, two decorative end papers that will wrap all the way around the dowels and still show 2" or more, two dowels

Use two dowels of the same diameter and length. Add knobs (drawer pulls) to the top and bottom of each.

steps 1 and 2

1. Hammer a 1" brad or nail into the center of the end of one of the dowels.
2. Put a dab of wood glue around the nail and into the hole in the end of the knob.
3. Hold the knob on top of the nail/dowel for a minute or two, until the glue sets.
4. Paint with acrylics when dry.

Attach your long "text" sheet to the decorative sheets at each end:

5. Run a line of PVA glue along the edge of the decorative sheet and glue the text sheet on top of it.
6. Glue the ends of the decorative sheets to the dowels. Glue them so the sheets wrap once around the dowels and the wood does not show.
7. To hang, add a decorative cord or ribbon at the top of the scroll.

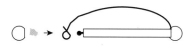

variation 1

Variation #1: Add the decorative cord or ribbon for hanging by attaching it at either end to the brads before gluing the knobs.
Variation #2: Sew together by machine instead of gluing.
Variation #3: Paint the text area with white gesso to create a nonporous writing or drawing surface.
Variation #4: Make knobs from colorful polymer clay instead of painted wood. Leave holes in the clay knobs so they can be glued around the nail and dowel.

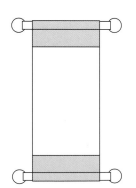

complete

Uses: amulet, housewarming scroll with good wishes, inspirational poem or quotation, biblical quote

Hanging Scroll with Attached Ribbons to Tie Closed

Follow the above directions, but glue the cover or decorative sheets to the dowels first. Leave about 1¹/₂ inches extra on the end of what will be the lower decorative sheet.

1. Make two slits on the right side and two on the left, one an inch above the other vertically. Make two slits on the right and left that are at least 1" from the outer edges.
2. Thread the ribbon from the back to the front through each pair of slits, and straighten the ends.
3. Glue the middle of the ribbon to the paper.
4. Glue the text sheet on top of the portion of the ribbon that is glued down to hide it. You should have two ribbons with four ends hanging out the back.

Variation: Sew by machine, attaching the ribbons as you join the decorative sheets and text.

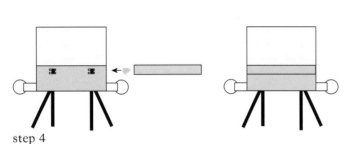

steps 1 and 2   step 4

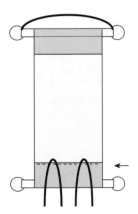

variation

Where We Put Our Hopes: Wishing Scroll, 1994, collagraphs, letterpress, acrylics and gesso, hanging scroll, 8¹/₂ x 20"

CHAPTER 4

Intermediate Compound Structures

 he following structures are combinations of bindings. A side-binding and a perfect binding merge, and the versatile accordion-fold gets some flags, signatures, or pockets. With rounded and tabbed signatures and an interwoven spine, the piano hinge is a marriage of cut pages and threaded sticks; its soft cover has an inner pop-up. Its alternate hard cover needs to be sewn. Refer to previous chapters to refresh your memory of the accordion-fold or single signature (pamphlet stitch) binding, or choose an appropriate cover from Chapter 7.

Side Binding with Glued Cover

Time: 30–45 minutes

I painted words on paper with acrylic inks, then painted over some of the words with gesso for the cover and page backs for *Ezra's Book.* Our son Ezra had to stay in the hospital for a week after he was born due to an unexpected heart condition. We brought him home on Valentine's Day, which makes the heart a more potent symbol for me. I wanted to make a book for him but didn't want it to be all about the terrible first week of his life since he was a happy, charming baby. So I wrote poems to celebrate him: his likes and dislikes, what excites him, and so on, and printed those poems on the pages. On the back I printed what happened to him and how we felt, but I printed it at the very edge, hidden near the binding, so the reader would have to hunt for it. Side-bound books don't open completely, which is why I chose this structure.

Ezra's Book, 1997, letterpress, acrylic inks and gesso, side-bound with glued cover, 11 x 5"

Adding interior sewing strengthens a glued, perfect-bound book. Use PVA only for the best results.

Materials: binder clip, bone folder, pencil, ruler, PVA, glue brush, needle, thread, awl or leather punch, scrap paper, waxed paper, cardboard to protect work surface

Example: $5^3/4$ x $8^3/4$" book

Paper: $1/4$" stack of paper, grained short, $5^1/2$ x $8^1/2$" (or pages with at least a $1^1/2$" left margin); heavier cover stock, $5^3/4$ x 18", grained short

To sew the pages:
1. Stack the pages in front of you, landscape orientation. Secure with a binder clip at the top edge, roughly 3" from the left side.
2. Measure in one inch from the left.
3. Score a line from head to tail.
4. Measure an inch from the head and tail and mark on the score line. Punch holes in these two places.
Sew from back to front as follows:
5. Up through the top hole; take the thread around the side and back up through the same hole.
6. Down through the bottom hole; take the thread around the side and back down through the bottom hole.
7. Tie the ends in a square knot and trim.

To fold the cover:
8. On the inside of the cover, measure $8^3/4$" from each end and score lines from head to tail. You should have a $1/4$" gap between the two scores that will be the spine.

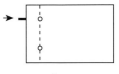

step 5

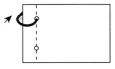

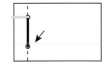

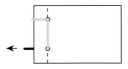

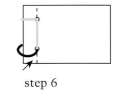

step 6

step 7

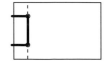

complete

9. On the outside of the cover, measure 7³/₄″ from each end and score lines from head to tail. These scores will help you open the book.

10. Fold at all the score lines. When the cover is open with the inside showing, the inside score lines will be valley folds and the outside folds will be peak folds.

To glue:

11. Place scrap paper on your work surface. Open the cover in front of you.

12. On the inside of the cover spread a thin layer of glue in the area from the leftmost fold to the rightmost. You may put glue on the spine of your book block at this point as well.

13. Nestle the book inside, align, and smooth down.

14. Wrap the entire book in waxed paper, and press under a heavy book overnight.

Uses: sketch book, ledger, poetry book, address book

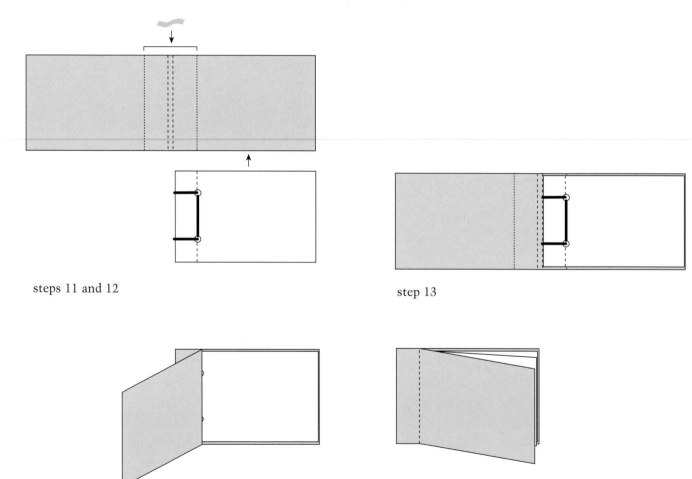

steps 11 and 12

step 13

complete interior view

complete

Accordion with Signatures
(folding & sewing)

Time: 30–60 minutes

Anne Schwartzburg and I used this wavelike structure for our book *Tidal Poems* because we wanted the reader to physically experience the flow of the tide. The poems are about water and the sea.

Tidal Poems (a collaboration with Anne Schwartzburg), 1995, letterpress, inks and watercolors, linoleum blocks, photoengravings of drawings by Schwartzburg, 10 x 11¹/₂"

Materials: knife, cutting mat, metal ruler, bone folder, thread, needles, awl, glue/paste, dishes for glue, glue brush, scrap paper, waxed paper

Example: 5¹/₂ x 5¹/₄" book

Paper: one sheet 5¹/₂ x 8", grained short (this will be the spine: the accordion or concertina); six to twelve sheets 5¹/₂ x 8¹/₂", grained short (these will be the signatures)

For this book we will make a one-inch accordion with three signatures on the peak fold.
1. Fold the spine paper in half. Open.
2. Fold the ends to the middle fold one end at a time.
3. Fold the ends back to the new folds, making sure they are aligned.
4. Turn the paper over, keeping everything folded.
5. Align the folded ends with the middle fold; crease. You should now have an accordion with alternating folds at every inch.

If two folded papers are needed, as for a book with more signatures:
1. Fold two accordions following the above instructions.
2. Cut off a one-inch segment from one sheet.
3. Place the uncut, 8" accordion in front of you, open. The first fold on the left should be a valley fold. Glue the accordion that you cut to the end of this one. Place the 7" accordion next to this one, facing opposite so that its first fold is a peak.
4. Apply glue in a thin, flat line to the front of the first one-inch segment of the 7" accordion.
5. Align completely with the first segment of the 8" accordion and smooth down. The final accordion should continually alternate valley and peak. To sew the book, the first and last folds should be valley folds.

For the signatures:
1. Fold all the paper for the signatures in half, widthwise. Group and nest the folded papers into three even piles (six for "doubled" accordion).
2. Mark each peak fold on the front with a light pencil mark. Refold these peaks into valleys for sewing. Align one signature with each mark; clip together temporarily with a binder clip.
3. With your needle, bodkin, or awl, poke three holes through the folds where you will sew. The holes go through each signature and its corresponding accordion fold. Leave at least $1/2$" from each end. (For help in making the holes at even intervals, see "Measuring for an Odd Number of Holes," in Chapter 2.)
4. Sew as for single signature/pamphlet stitch (see Chapter 2).
5. Refold the marked valleys back into peaks.
6. Place waxed paper between parts of the accordion and its pages that have been glued together (if applicable).
7. Press under heavy book overnight (not necessary if you did no gluing).
8. Add covers (choose from Chapter 7): wrapped hard cover ($1/4$" taller than the pages, the width of the spine plus the width of the pages plus $1/4$", that is $5^3/4$ x $5^1/2$" in this example), adhesive hard cover with hinged spine, or cover separate boards.

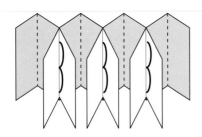

complete

Notes: If you choose to use the hinged hard cover, make your accordion out of a light-weight paper. As with most accordion-style books, this book expands when you open it. It will not open as much with a hinged hard cover. The signatures are connected only to the accordion spine, not to each other.

Variation: Sew the signatures in the valley folds. The dimensions of the boards for a hard cover would be $5^1/2$ x $4^1/2$" in this example.

Uses: three (or six) separate stories or sets of text; series of photos of three (or six) connected people, places, or things

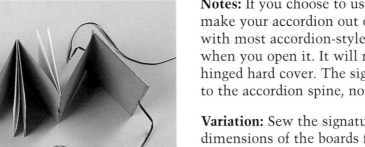

Accordion with signatures (in valley folds), 1996, blank book, $4^1/2$ x $5^3/4$"

Pocket Book
(folding & gluing)

Time: 30–60 minutes

Vicky Lee showed me a blank book with this structure that she had purchased at a calligraphy fair. After studying it, I figured out how to make one.

Eight Degrees of Charity, by Maimonides, based on 12th century text, artist's book made in 1995, letterpress, linoleum cuts, pocket book, 2¹/₂ x 2¹/₄"

The pockets contain the pieces of a double-sided puzzle in the book *Eight Degrees of Charity.* Since the author, Moses Ben Maimon (Maimonides), lived in the 12th century, I wanted the book to reflect the style of binding used at that time. Dominic Riley, a fine bookbinder in Berkeley, California, kindly lent me information about 12th century books, some of which was based on his own research. The old book probably would have had a wooden cover and been sewn to cords. For protection it likely had a cover or "chemise" with pockets. A clasp would have held together the springy parchment signatures. I used elements of a 12th century book—woodlike veneer paper for the covers, pockets, a clasp (a bone closure, in this case)—but did not set out to literally copy the historical binding. The copper hand is for decoration, but readers often try to undo the book by pulling on it. I liked the hand charm and didn't want to omit it, even to avoid confusion. I found good historical information in *The Coming of the Book: The Impact of Printing,* by Lucien Febvre and Henri-Jean Martin, and *The Art and History of Books,* by Norma Levarie.

Note: Use care and work slowly when you fold the accordion over the pockets. It is easy to make unwanted wrinkles.

Materials: bone folder, knife and cutting mat, PVA glue, glue brush, scissors, pencil, metal ruler (24" is helpful), scrap paper, waxed paper

Example: 5$^1/_2$ x 8" book with 4" pockets

Paper: two soft, light-weight, inner papers, 12 x 24". Make sure you cut the paper with the grain short.

1. Cut off an inch from one of the papers, making it 12 x 23".
2. Mark, score, and fold both long papers at 4" (to make them long and skinny). These 4" will be the pockets. It helps to fold this long fold against a 24" metal ruler, holding the ruler next to the score and folding up.
3. On the 24" sheet of paper, fold back an inch from the right edge, making a peak fold (the plain sides should be touching). The tab (folded inch) should be on the right. The pocket should be on the bottom.
4. Optional: "Shape" the horizontal pocket edges at this time (diagonals, curves, diamonds, etc.) by unfolding again and cutting the edge to the desired shape with a knife or decorative scissors.
5. Fold the paper in half, widthwise, to where you folded the tab, backs together, pocket-side-up.
6. Fold the edges back in half (pocket-side-in) to the first fold to create an accordion with three folds (plus the tab).
7. Repeat the accordion fold for the 23" paper (no tab).
8. Glue the pocket edge of the tab down to its parent paper.
9. Glue the complete tab to the back of the other paper. Glue the edges of the exposed pocket on the end. Glue down the very edges of the end pockets to the parent sheet if you will not have a cover.
10. Add a soft, open spine cover or separate wrapped hard covers (see Chapter 7 on covers). If you make a hard cover with separate boards you may wish to trim the edges of the end pockets so they won't be so bulky under the endsheets (see the diagram on page 119).

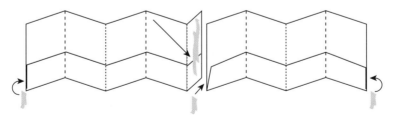

steps 1, 2, 3, and 5, 6, 7, 8, 9

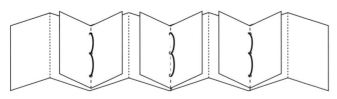

variation

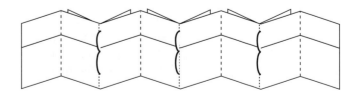

variation (opposite side)

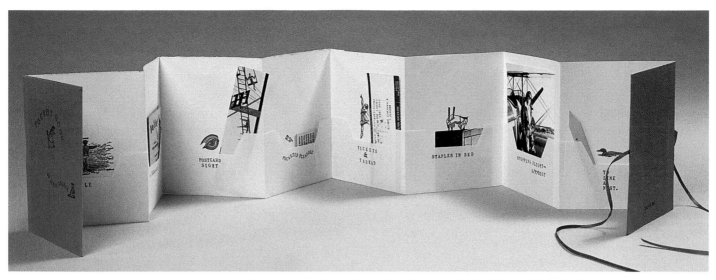

Pocket Book, 1995, rubber stamps, found objects, 5 x 6¹/₂"

Note: When you make a cover, you lose the front and last pockets (yielding six pockets), but I think a cover makes this book complete.

Variation: Add three signatures, one in each of the valley folds on the side opposite the pockets.

Uses: scrapbook, business card holder, booklet of stationery, postcard collection, photograph wallet. Write personal text on the folded papers placed in the pockets for an intimate reading experience.

Flag Book
(folding and gluing)

Time: 30–60 minutes

The flag book pops open in a surprising way. Betsy Davids taught me how to make this structure after showing the class Susan King's *Women and Cars*. The cards in Susan's book open to create one complete photograph. The structure is usually credited to Hedi Kyle, who was one of the first people to teach interesting, non-traditional structures.

I made *before woman was fin* in a class I taught with Nan Wishner. She photocopied and cut out lots of words. Each student got an envelope with a select few words. We arranged the words to make phrases. After gluing the phrases to cards, we attached the cards to the accordion.

The Lending Library, 1996, letterpress, mixed media, accordion with library pockets, 3³/₄ x 6³/₄"

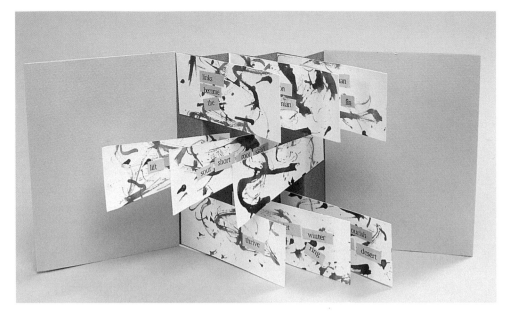

before woman was fin, 1996, acrylic inks, collage of found words, accordion with flags, 4¹/₂ x 6"

Marilyn A. Hatch, one of the special-collections librarians at Wellesley College, who teaches a book arts lab, made a flag book for the Wellesley College Alumnae Achievement Awards' 25th Anniversary Celebration. The flags in that book were long, narrow strips of various paste-papers with the name of the award recipient, year of graduation, and subject of the award (opera singer, dancer, etc.) letterpress-printed on them. The structure, open, looked like ripples of multicolored water. The book incorporated 95 flags: five on a peak fold, multiplied by 19 folds. Paste-papers are made by mixing a pigment or paint and a paste, such as methylcellulose. The paint/paste is spread over a full sheet of paper, then various combs are dragged over the surface to make designs.

Materials: glue brush, ruler, bone folder, scrap paper, PVA glue and containers

Example: 4¹/₄ x 5¹/₂" book with 9 cards

Paper: 8 x 5¹/₂" paper for spine accordion, grained short; nine cards, 1¹/₂ x 4¹/₄", grained short

To make eight 1" accordion segments:

1. Fold the paper in half, widthwise. Open.
2. Fold the ends to the middle fold, one end at a time.
3. Fold the ends back to the new folds, making sure they are aligned.
4. Turn the paper over, keeping everything folded.
5. Align the folded ends with the middle fold; crease. You should now have an accordion with alternating folds at every inch.
6. Face the accordion with its opening to the right.

Note: Glue the top and bottom cards down first, because they are on the same side of the fold. Then turn the "page" and glue the middle card so that there is space between all the cards. Although it looks tricky, just remember to ***apply glue to the back of the cards only***. Also, you don't need much glue. You are only attaching about 1" of the card to the accordion. Two cards have glue on the back right margin; the middle one has glue on the back left margin only.

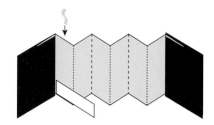

step 2

Glue cards in a row on each fold as follows:

1. Open the first flap. Put a thin coat of glue on the back of the first card (landscape orientation) on the right 1" margin only. Align the card with the top of the accordion on the front of the first peak fold, pushing the left edge of the card all the way into the valley fold.

2. Glue the second card, aligning it with the bottom of the accordion on the front of the first fold, also aligned with the valley fold.

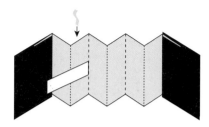

step 3

3. Glue the third card, lining it up under first card but gluing it to the back of the same fold. Remember, the glue is on the back of the card. It will look as though the image faces the opposite direction. Don't worry.

4. Continue the same pattern on all the folds, aligning all middle cards with the previous cards as well.

5. The pages/cards should end up all the same length. Trim if necessary.

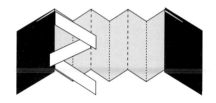

steps 1–3

6. Make an open spine cover or cover separate boards (see Chapter 7). A wrapped hard cover doesn't work well unless you glue the end tabs of the accordion inside the wrapped hard cover, which defeats the original concept of that particular cover: no glue. However, the point of this book is that you are free to choose the projects you like, and you are encouraged to customize each structure.

Variation #1: Make the covers connected to the accordion by using a longer paper (17 x 5¹/₂"). For nine cards you need 6" for the accordion in the middle. Measure 4¹/₂" from each edge. Score and fold. Then fold the accordion in the center of the long paper by aligning the folds and creasing.

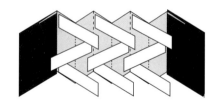

steps 3–6

Variation #2: Make larger cards from heavy black paper. Mount photographs on them.

Variation #3: Glue two or three accordions together to make room for 18 or 30 cards. If you use an even number of accordions, you must cut off the end flap for the book to be properly oriented; hence, 18 cards. (See "Accordion with Signatures," page 76, for directions about gluing accordions together.)

Uses: book of sayings, photo display album, collaborative project, definitions of one word, birthday book, business card holder, postcard display, honor roll list (one name per strip)

Accordion with flags photo album, 1996, acrylic and gesso cards, 8 x 11"

Piano Hinge with Skewers
(cutting, weaving)

Time: 40–60 minutes

The signatures in this structure are woven together over sticks, instead of sewn. When the book is held horizontally it creates an object like a library newspaper holder. Soft covers work with little pop-up-like folds inside and look similar to the pages. Hard covers are fastened with a modified side-binding. Create a holder or horizontal slipcase to house the piano-hinge book because the skewers cause the book to sit at an angle. When Adele Crawford took my class, she sewed old recipes to the pages, letting the thread-ends hang out of the book; it looked great. The structure is usually attributed to Hedi Kyle. It also appears in *Non-Adhesive Binding: Books Without Paste or Glue,* by Keith A. Smith, and *Cover to Cover,* by Shereen LaPlantz. I modified the covers.

Piano hinges, 1997, with hard cover, acrylic inks, 4¹/₄ x 5", slipcase, 5 x 6 x 1¹/₂", red softcover, with offcuts from *Ezra's Book*, 4¹/₄ x 4"

Materials: pencil, knife and cutting mat or scissors, bamboo skewers, macramé cord or ribbon, awl, ruler, needle, bone folder, PVA glue and brush, scrap paper

Example: 5 x 4¹/₄" book with five "tabs"

Text pages: photocopies or handwritten pages of recipes, or use a glue stick or sew, machine-stitch to the paper recipes, ingredients, a memorable feast, guest checks, or lists of favorite foods, etc.

Paper: fifteen or more 8½ x 5" sheets, grained short; decorative, colored paper as section cover-dividers, if desired

Note: The photos show books with six sections, each of which uses three inner sheets per section (18 per book) plus the decorative dividers (six per book).

steps 2, 3, 4

1. Group pages evenly into three or more sections, with 2–4 inner sheets per section and one decorative sheet face-up on the top of each. Do not fold in half.

Proceed as follows:

2. Pick up one section and center it to wrap around the skewer.
3. Wrap it, bringing the fore edge ends together and smoothing toward the skewer/spine with the bone folder.
4. Mark horizontal lines, evenly spaced (four, in this example, 1" apart) along this semi-crease. Lines should extend evenly, the width of your skewer (or dowel or pencil, if you use those instead) on both sides of the skewer/spine.

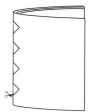

5. With scissors, using the end of each line as the tip of your triangle, cut small equilateral triangles (³⁄₈–¹⁄₄" for skewers, ¹⁄₂" if you use pencils). Or open the section and cut small diamonds with a knife. Take care to wrap and crease each subsequent section like the first one. Cut all triangles. Now you have created tabs between the triangles.

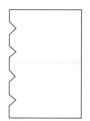

step 5

6. Bend the odd tabs one way (let's say to the left) and the even tabs the other way (right). Your tabs should alternate sides.
7. Repeat for all sections.
8. Fit all sections together. Link one section to the next (the tabs from one should nestle over the tabs from the next).
9. Insert a skewer by poking the pointed end vertically through the center of the tabs. The spine will look woven.
10. Repeat until all the sections are linked.
11. Trim off the pointed ends if you like.

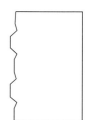

step 6

Covers for the Piano Hinge

For soft covers: To attach a soft cover to the front and back sections, you will need medium- to heavy-weight cover paper that will be folded in half. For this example use two sheets 5 x 9½", grained short.

1. Measure, mark, and score ³⁄₄", 1", 1¹⁄₄" on the back from the right edge of the front cover and the left edge of the back cover. You should have three scores, each ¹⁄₄" apart.
2. For the moment, valley-fold only the 1" flap, wrong sides together.

3. Measure and cut triangles on this fold as you did for the sections.

4. Bend tabs, alternating left and right. Then, open and smooth out.

5. For the front cover, push in any tabs that would otherwise bend right, by opening and refolding, like an accordion or inner pop-up with a middle valley fold, one peak fold on either side. You will connect only the left tabs.

6. For the back cover, push in the opposite tabs because you will connect the cover to the text block with only the right tabs.

7. Apply PVA to the cover pieces on both sides of the inner pop-up and along the edge flap to glue the cover to itself. Press down.

8. To complete, thread a skewer through the covers and the text block.

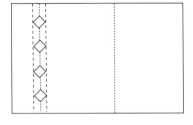

step 1

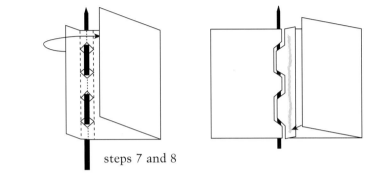

steps 7 and 8

Variation: Make a hard cover instead. Use museum boards that are 1/4" narrower than the book block. Poke holes and sew loops around the skewer in place of the tabs that would face to the left. See "Stick Binding" or "Side-Bound Book" for sewing ideas.

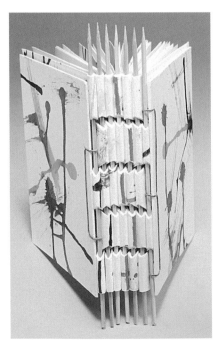

Piano hinge, hard cover

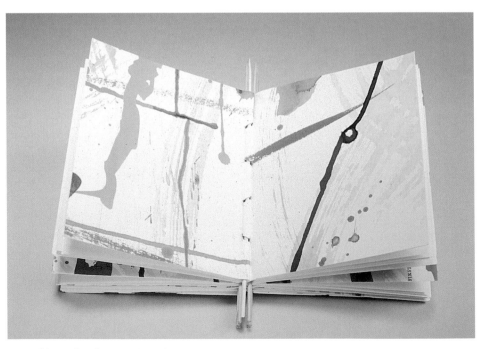

Piano hinge, hard cover, interior

CHAPTER 5

Multiple Signatures or Thick Sewn Books

he following books are variations on the Western multiple signature binding, except the chain stitch. Each book has several signatures or gatherings of pages nested one inside the other and an almost identical sewing pattern. The books look different, however. In some cases the stitching is attractive and meant to be visible. In other cases it merely holds the book together and is covered with something more decorative.

I include the chain stitch here because it, too, includes several signatures (at least six to make the decorative stitching apparent). Unlike the other books, the stitches must attach to the covers as you sew, and a curved needle is necessary. Because the sewing is the only support for this book, keep the dimensions small. Covers can be any rigid material you are able to punch or drill holes into (museum board, plexiglass, wood, metal). Curved needles (also known as quilters' needles) are available at most fabric stores. I like using waxed macramé thread for this structure.

You may wish to refer to "Measuring for an Odd Number of Holes," in Chapter 2, page 42.

Knots for Multiple Signatures

You will also need to know the square knot (see page 42).

Kettle Stitch

This makes a half-hitch knot. Use the kettle stitch whenever you have more than two signatures to sew together.

1. Take the needle from the outside to inside between the preceding signatures. See the diagram.

step 1

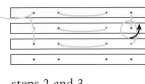
step 2

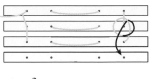
steps 2 and 3

step 3

step 2

step 3

2. Don't pull the thread all the way into another stitch, but leave a loop.

3. Cross over the thread, and draw the needle through the loop.

French Knot or Double Knot

The French knot is a variation of the half-hitch knot.

1. Take the needle from the outside to the inside between the preceding signatures.

2. Don't pull the thread all the way into another stitch, but leave a loop.

3. Cross over the thread and draw the needle through the loop. Don't tighten it yet. Cross over the thread again and draw the needle through the loop.

4. Gently hold the knot down to the hole in the book as you tighten it.

Calculating Thread

Generally, the length of thread is measured by holding its end to one end hole, drawing it to the last hole and multiplying by the number of signatures, then adding six more inches total to tie off each end. For some reason, my measurement always comes out to 18–24 inches. Sometimes the directions say "four times the width or sewing side of your book."

Western Multiple Signature

Time: 10–25 minutes

The multiple signature is the most common binding.

Materials: knife, cutting mat, scissors, metal ruler, bone folder, thread, needle, awl, 16 inner pages to make a book 4¹/₄ x 5¹/₂" (from 8¹/₂ x 11" cut in half and folded)

Two-Hole

For practice, begin with two holes only.

1. Fold all pages in half.
2. Nest four pages inside one another. Make four sets of four.
3. Stack up with the folded edges aligned.
4. Put the stacked signatures flat on the table with the spines facing you.
5. Measure 1" from each end; draw vertical lines, so that you mark all four folds at these two places.
6. With a knife, cut a groove along the pencil marks. You have just made sewing holes that should be aligned.
7. Keep the signatures stacked, spines aligned and facing you. Start on the outside at the top signature. Go in one hole, and leave a tail of about 3" (something you can tie off easily).
8. Go out the other hole in that signature. Pick up the next signature, and go from out to in on the corresponding hole.
9. Come out the top hole and tie it tightly in a square knot to the end remaining.
10. Go in and out the third signature. At this end do a kettle stitch: take the needle between the signatures and out, drawing the needle through the loop and making a half-hitch knot.
11. Proceed with the remaining signatures, always making a kettle stitch to the preceding signature if that end would otherwise remain unattached.
12. To finish, make a last kettle stitch and tie off with a square knot.
13. Make a wrapped hard cover or a hard cover for multiple signatures. See Chapter 7.

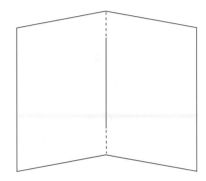

inside view of one signature

I used the multiple signature for my first book, *never mind the crowd*, but mistakenly sewed with waxed macramé thread, which is too thick; it created wide gaps between the signatures. I chose to use the macramé thread for

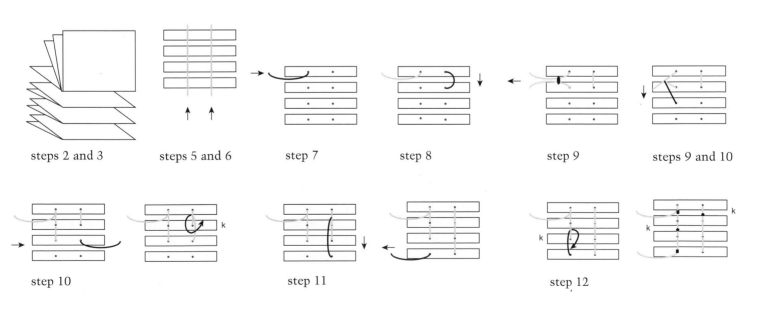

steps 2 and 3   steps 5 and 6   step 7   step 8   step 9   steps 9 and 10

step 10   step 11   step 12

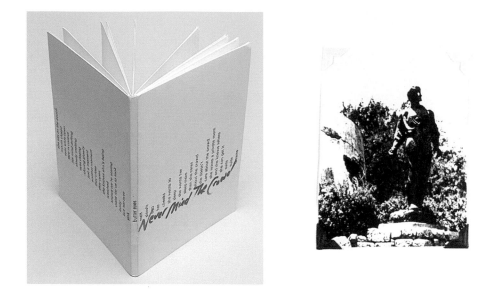

Left: *never mind the crowd*, 1983, letterpress, photocopy, multiple signatures, 4⁷/₈ x 7"
Right: *never mind the crowd*, interior

Cinnamon and Saffron, 1997, letterpress on paper custom made by David Kimball at Magnolia Editions, acrylic painted cover, linoleum cut labels, 3¹/₂ x 5"

Cinnamon & Saffron because it is available in that great yellow-orange squash color. To make the gaps less obvious, I glued a strip of paper over the spine that matched the text paper. When Nan Wishner went to France, she found squash names in French. Inside the book, I included two squash recipes as well as a short story, and devised vegetable labels printed in English and French. *Cinnamon & Saffron* is a romantic comedy of love and squash.

Four-Hole

1. Assemble signatures, mark the spines, and slit or make holes as for two holes, adding an even number to make four, six, or more holes (in this case, four).

2. Stack the signatures as before, spines aligned and facing you.

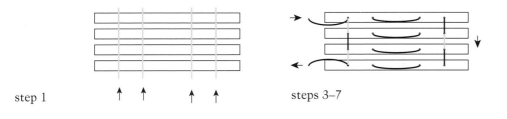

step 1   steps 3–7

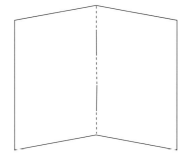

inside view

Sewing Pattern: Thread the needle with five times the length of the book.

3. Start on the outside at the top signature. Go in and out that signature, then in and out again with a running stitch.

4. Go into the next signature, and sew a running stitch again.

5. When you finish that signature, tie it tightly to the remaining tail of thread.

6. Sew the third signature. When you complete the third, do a kettle stitch.

7. Proceed until the last signature. Make another kettle stitch, then tie off in a square knot.

8. Make a wrapped hard cover or hard cover for multiple signatures. (See Chapter 7, pages 108 and 118.)

Multiple Signature onto a Ribbon

Time: 15–20 minutes to sew and 10–15 minutes to make cover

Michael's mother gave me some Nigerian cloth that became the book *Lizard's Snake Suit* instead of curtains. I thought I might make a book for her; maybe I'd make a recipe book or guest book. But, after studying the animals in the pattern of the cloth, I realized I had to write a story about them. Michael said jokingly, "Lizard got up and put on his suit." My eyes lit up, and I scribbled out *Lizard's Snake Suit*. I was inspired by a structure in *Cover to Cover*, by Shereen LaPlantz. Ribbons add immediate color to the outside of this book.

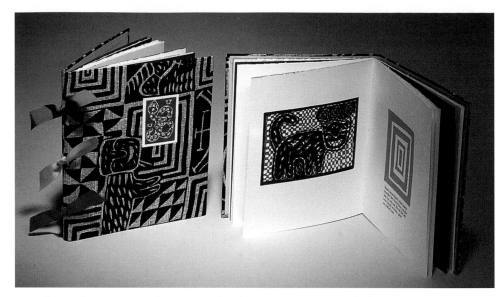

Lizard's Snake Suit, 1996, letterpress, linoleum cuts, Nigerian cloth, multiple signatures around ribbon, inset title block, 9 x 11"

Materials: knife, cutting mat, scissors, metal ruler, needle, thread, pencil, bone folder; two ribbons, 1/2–1" wide, each a minimum of 6" long (long enough to tie in a knot or bow)

Example: 4^1/$_2$ x 5^3/$_4$" book with two ribbons

Paper: sixteen sheets, 8^1/$_2$ x 5^1/$_2$", grained short
  1. Fold the paper in half, dividing the pages by the number of signatures you will use (in this example, four).
  2. Stack the sheets into four signatures, fold-side facing you.
  3. Measure 1/2" from each end; with a pencil, draw vertical lines, marking all four signatures at these two places. These are the holes at the head and tail. Between the head and tail holes, measure for four more holes: one set of two holes for each ribbon. Each pair of marks should be spaced just slightly farther apart than the width of the ribbon you are using. For a 1/2" wide ribbon, measuring from the head, you can make marks at 1^1/$_2$", 1^{13}/$_{16}$", 3^{11}/$_{16}$", and 4". With a pencil, mark vertically down all the folded spines again.

Note: No matter how many ribbons you use, you will need an even number of holes, always with two free holes at the head and tail. With two ribbons you need six holes. If you want three ribbons, you need three sets of holes plus the two at the ends, or eight holes.
  4. Poke the six holes in the fold of each signature with your needle. Or use the knife to make nicks in the folds alone the lines.

Sewing pattern:
  5. Start the needle from the outside of the first signature using the end hole.

6. Sew as for a multiple-signature binding, threading the ribbon through its loops after you sew two signatures (otherwise, it will fall out).

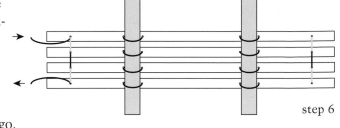

step 6

If you make a hard cover:
7. Once your boards are covered and dried, center the book block (the sewn signatures) on the spine on the inside. Mark lightly with a pencil where the ribbons will go.
  8. Make parallel slits on each side of the spine for each ribbon.
  9. Thread the ribbons through the slits from inside to outside.
10. Tie outside, on the spine, in bow or square knot.

Variation: As you sew the last signature, put a loop around each stitch that holds a ribbon and knot. (Use if you make a book with four or more signatures.)

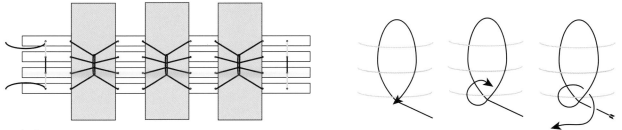

variation

Uses: wedding book, journal, guest book, sketch book

Exposed Stitch
(folding and sewing)

Time: 30–45 minutes

Sew directly to a heavy paper cover or sew to a spine piece and glue to boards for one of the hard covers, keeping the sewing exposed or covering (see "Split Board," page 114). For this binding you need an even number of holes. A larger book might have six or eight. Variations of this structure appear in *Non-Adhesive Bindings*, by Keith A. Smith.

Materials: pencil, ruler, needle, thread, bone folder, knife, cutting mat

Cover: $5^3/4$ x $9^1/4$" heavy paper. The cover or wrapper should be the width of your pages, opened, plus the depth of the signatures stacked up (in this example, four signatures stacked should measure approximately $1/2$").
Text or inner paper: Sixteen papers $5^1/2$ x $8^1/2$", grained short.

Exposed stitch models, 1997, acrylic inks and gesso, waxed linen thread, blank books, green with white pages, 4^1/$_2$ x 6", purple with pink pages, 4^1/$_2$ x 5^7/$_8$"

1. Fold all the pages in half widthwise.
2. Nest four pages inside one another. Make four sets of four.
3. Stack up with the folded edges aligned, fold-side facing you. Measure ^{1}/$_2$" from the head and tail; with a pencil mark vertically down all the signatures.
4. Poke the four holes in the fold with your needle. Or notch all the signatures at once with a knife.

Prepare the cover:
5. Find the middle of your cover paper (don't fold it, just lightly mark it with a pencil).
6. If your book block is approximately ^{1}/$_2$" deep, measure ^{1}/$_4$" on each side of your tiny midline pencil mark. Mark these two spots, top and bottom (head and tail).
7. Score these two lines with a bone folder against a rule. Fold. Open.
8. Line up the signatures within the cover. Mark along the spine of the cover exactly where the holes are in the signatures. Make a straight line from fold to fold horizontally across the spine of the cover, wherever the four marks are. Make four horizontal slits on the pencil marks.
9. You will be sewing your signatures through these slits.

To sew:

10. Starting with one signature, hold it inside the cover, the holes of the signature aligned with the slits in the cover. With an arm's length, or approximately 20", of thread, begin sewing from the outside of the cover, through the slit, through the end hole of the first signature. Leave a 4" tail.

11. Sew now from the inside of the signature, through the next slit, then in the next slit, and through the signature, creating a running stitch.

12. At the end of the first signature, make a French knot (double knot).

13. Line up the second signature with the slit, and continue sewing a running stitch.

14. At the end of the second signature make a French knot (double knot). **Tip:** As you make the knot, hold the loop down on the book, as close to the hole as possible, as you slowly tighten the thread all the way.

15. Sew back down the third signature.

16. When you get to the end, make a kettle stitch under the previous French knot; then, make a second double knot.

17. Sew the fourth signature.

18. Make a kettle stitch at the end and a double knot; then, take your needle through the same end hole back inside the cover. Remove the needle.

19. Rethread the first end through the needle, and take the thread back inside the cover through the first hole.

20. Pull the two ends around and tie together in a square knot. Trim.

Variation: The cover may also have edge flaps that will be turned in (folded in); these should be at minimum half the width of the cover (this size would need two $2^{1}/_{8}$" flaps). $8^{1}/_{2}$" + $^{1}/_{2}$" + [2 × ($2^{1}/_{8}$")] = minimum wrapper paper = $13^{1}/_{4}$". (Maximum flap measurement can be the same width, or [2 × ($4^{1}/_{4}$")] = $8^{1}/_{2}$" totaling: $17^{1}/_{2}$" maximum wrapper paper needed.)

Uses: journal or travel journal, sketch book

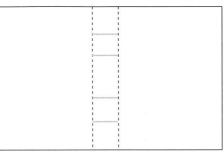

steps 6–9

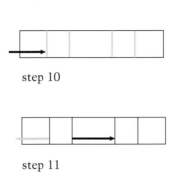

step 10

step 11

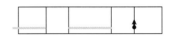

steps 12

step 13

step 14

step 14

step 15

step 16

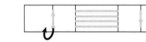

step 17

step 18

step 19

step 20

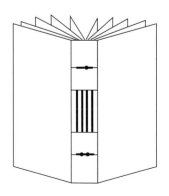

Chain Stitch
(folding, sewing)

Time: 30–40 minutes

This traditional book has a flexible spine, unsupported by paper or boards. Make it small; or add more holes to support a larger book. I was inspired to learn this binding after seeing Elsi Vassdal Ellis's miniature, *Dear El Lissitzky*. Her book, with a slightly different, Ethiopian binding, employed a technique with two needles, I believe. An unsupported spine works well on a miniature book.

Materials: knife, cutting mat, ruler, pencil, awl, waxed macramé or other waxed thread, curved needle

Example: $5^3/_4$ x $4^1/_2$" book

Paper: fifteen to twenty-eight $5^1/_2$ x $8^1/_2$" pages, grained short; two $5^3/_4$ x $4^1/_2$" boards, grained long

  1. Fold the $5^1/_2$ x $8^1/_2$" pieces in half. Nest into sets (signatures) of three to four pages per signature. Make five to seven signatures.
  2. Stack the signatures, one atop the other, with the spines facing you. Measure for three holes along the spines, leaving at least $1/_4$" but no more than $1/_2$" from (what will be) the top and bottom edges. You can just mark one of your signatures, then put it back atop the others.
  3. With the stack even, draw straight lines down the folds where you marked the first signatures, so that when you sew, the signatures will align.

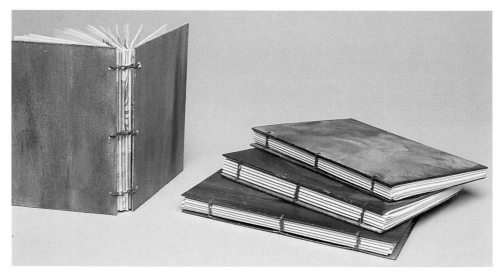

Chain stitch, blank books, 1996, orange with offcuts from *Onion:* 3 x $4^1/_8$", teal: 4 x 5", red: 4 x 5", silver: $4^1/_4$ x $5^1/_2$"

4. Poke holes with your needle at these lines on each signature, taking care to keep the orientation the same so the signatures will still align when you put them back together.

5. Poke three holes in your cover boards as well, 1/4" from the left (front board) and 1/4" from the right (back board).

6. Place the boards, top and bottom aligned, to surround your signatures.

7. Treating the top board and the first signature as one unit, pick these up.

Begin to sew as follows:

8. Thread a needle with a length of waxed thread that is the height of the book (from head to tail) multiplied by the number of signatures.

9. Start at the end hole from inside the first signature. Leave a tail of about three inches.

10. Come out through the first hole on the board from the inside, then come back through the same first hole in the signature again.

11. Sew to the second hole in the signature, come out, go through the second hole in the cover, and go back through the second hole in the s ignature.

12. For the last hole, go out the signature and through the board, but instead of going through the third hole in the first signature, sew through the last hole in the second signature.

13. Go out the middle hole of the second signature. Here's the chain part: take your needle under the stitch between the board and the first signature. (Don't try to go between the loop; go under both ends of the loop.) Then go back in the middle hole of the second signature.

14. Proceed to the third hole, going under the last stitch between the first signature and the board. Instead of going back into the third hole, add the third signature and go in the last hole there.

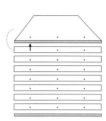

step 9

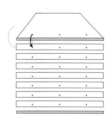

step 10

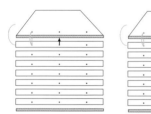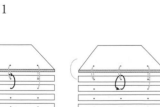

step 11

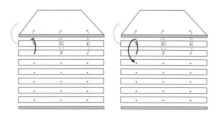

step 12

step 13

step 14

 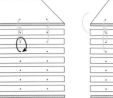  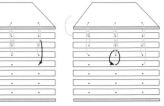

step 15

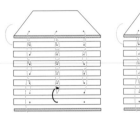 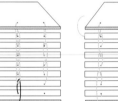

15. Repeat this pattern with the rest of the signatures, making sure that when you get to the last signature you pick up the last board with it. Sew from the outside of the board, make a loop, and then go through the last hole of the last signature from the outside to the inside.

16. Come out the middle hole of the signature, go from the inside to the outside through the middle hole of the board, loop under the middle stitch between the two previous signatures, and go back into the middle hole of the current signature.

17. Sew out the last hole of the signature, from the inside to the outside of the board loop and back through the last hole of the signature. Make a half-hitch or kettle stitch with your remaining thread to the stitch inside the last signature. Tie off the first stitch in the first signature as well.

  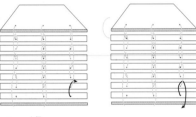

step 16   step 17

Variation #1: First, quickly paint both sides of your two boards, using acrylic paints sparingly, straight from the tube or squeezed out onto a paper towel with no water added. Paint the edges as well. The boards should dry within a few minutes.

Variation #2: Glue decorative paper to the front and back of the boards, wrap in waxed paper, and press under a heavy weight overnight before sewing.

Uses: travel journal, guest book, scrapbook, photo album, text about things that are linked

the phone visit from the next, 1996, collage with color photocopy from *A Book in the Garden,* Book One of *A Garden Variety Book,* reshuffled text from *The Local Desk,* Book Two from *The Lending Library,* chain stitch, 3³/4 x 2"

Jacob's Ladders

The Jacob's ladder is a traditional child's toy, but it has characteristics of a book. You interact with it at your own pace. It is movable. It has a sequence. It opens and closes, and it has front and back covers. I saw Paddy Thornbury's Jacob's ladder in *Cover to Cover*, then spent several hours trying to figure out how to make one. The structure calls out for words that will appear and disappear as the book moves. I'd like to make one as a baby book with photos of a child at different ages, thus depicting the child growing up or "moving through time."

Two-Panel with (or without) Cards

Time: 15–30 minutes

Bonnie Thompson Norman, a fellow teacher and book artist, introduced me to the Jacob's ladder with cards. She sent me one that her students had created called *The Army Cook Kissed My Sister*. I was baffled for an hour until I realized just how the pages turned. I include the instructions for reading the book after the directions for making it. This variation is particularly fun when words are written on each of a set of cards. The words could be found poetry or an existing poem or sentence, cut up.

Materials: PVA glue or glue/paste mixture, glue brush, scrap paper, scissors

Example: $4^1/_2$ x $5^3/_4$" finished size, using 36" of ribbon, with six cards

Paper: four 4-ply boards cut to the same size, all grained the same way (these may be painted, collaged, or covered first)
$1/_8$–$1/_4$" ribbon approximately six times the width of one board
Six cards $1/_4$–$1/_2$" smaller than the board

1. Cut ribbon into thirds.
2. Line up your boards in pairs, covers on the bottom.

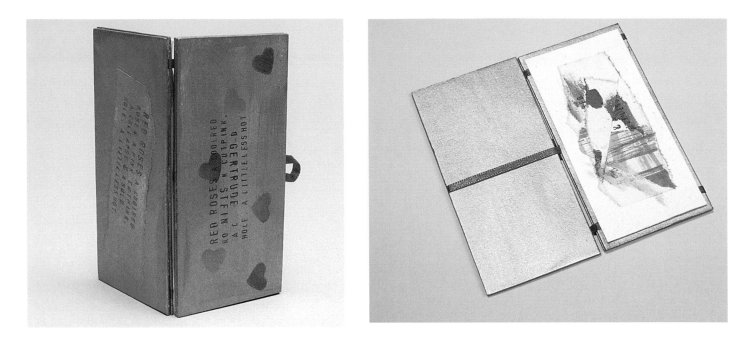

Left: *Gertrude Stein Valentine: Red Roses* (cover), 1997, acrylics, collage, rubber stamps, one of four copies, 2 x 4"
Right: *Gertrude Stein Valentine* (interior)

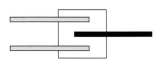

step 4

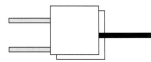

step 5

3. Brush a thin layer of glue in the middle on the back of the first inside (non-cover) board.

4. Glue down an inch of each one of three ribbons as follows: one ribbon facing right, centered, and the other two ribbons facing left, top and bottom (about 1/4" from head and tail).

5. Take the front cover, and apply glue completely to the back of it.

6. Glue it down to the first board, sandwiching the ribbons.

7. Flip the book over so the front cover is face-down (the middle ribbon is now facing left and the two ribbons right).

8. Put the back cover face-down next to the first "sandwich."

9. Pull the middle ribbon over to the right.

10. Put a line of glue, centered on the back of the back cover.

11. Glue down the middle ribbon.

12. Trim the end so the ribbon doesn't stick off the edge of the board, or double it and glue down the end of the ribbon to make a hanging loop.

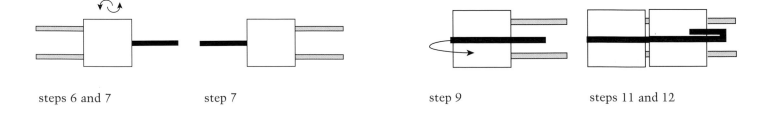

steps 6 and 7   step 7   step 9   steps 11 and 12

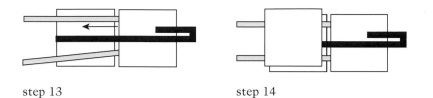

step 13   step 14   steps 16, 17, 18, 19

13. Pull out the top and bottom ribbons to the left.

14. Place the inside back panel face-down on top of the ribbon.

15. Put two lines of glue on this inside board.

16. Glue down the top and bottom ribbons.

17. Trim the ribbons so that when they are glued down the ends do not stick out from between the boards.

18. Apply glue completely on top of this board and the ribbons you just glued down.

19. Glue this panel on top of the back cover, sandwiching all the ribbons.

20. Put waxed paper around it and place it under a heavy book overnight. If you are using straight PVA, this step may not be necessary. Check to make sure the boards are securely glued if you decide not to put the book under a weight.

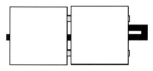

interior view complete

How the cards work:

Open the book. Place one card at a time on the right-hand side, on top of the ribbon. Close the book. Open it from the other edge. You will have to pull. Don't worry, you aren't tearing anything. The card should get caught up under the ribbon. Repeat for all cards, opening and closing the book from alternating edges. The cards should stack up three to a side. Eventually all the cards will be trapped under the ribbons. When you want to read or interact with this book again, slide the cards out carefully from under the ribbons, shuffle or arrange, and read again.

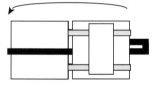

exterior complete

Six-Panel Book with Boards and Ribbon

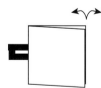

Time: 45–90 minutes

When I decided I wanted to make a book with this structure, I knew the book had to have a reference to a ladder in the text. I started with the biblical story of Jacob and his dream about angels ascending and descending a ladder. I thought about angels and flying. Flying in dreams is something Val told me she does naturally; I thought it would be fun to fly, too. So for many nights I thought about flying before I went to sleep. Finally, I could fly in my dreams. Then, in waking life I climbed a tall ladder. I broke out

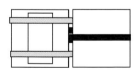

Fly on a Ladder, 1996, letterpress from zinc plate, 2¹/₂ x 2³/₄"

in a sweat; I discovered I was afraid of heights. That experience ended my dream-flying. *Fly on a Ladder* contains Jacob's story on one side and mine on the other.

A hand-sized (2¹/₂–3¹/₂") version of this book is pleasant to hold, but any size will work. I recommend two ribbons the same color for the top and bottom and a third, contrasting one for the middle, but any combination will do.

Tips: When you glue the ribbons, try to align them as you go. Glue the ribbons near the center, not too close to the top and bottom edges or they may slip out. The boards should be almost touching, with not too much space between the "sandwiches."

Materials: PVA glue or glue/paste mixture, glue brush, scrap paper, scissors, pencil, ruler

Paper: Twelve boards: 4-ply museum board is nice, all the same size and the grain going the same way.

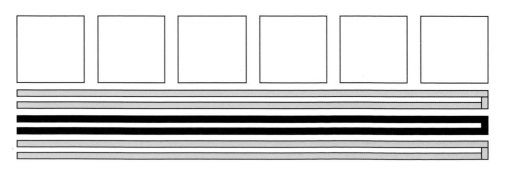

Three ribbons, $1/8$–$1/4$" wide, each ribbon two times the length of six boards in a row, just barely touching.

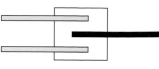

1. Glue down the ends (approximately 2") of the three ribbons to the back of the first board (not the front cover, but the inside cover). The middle ribbon faces right; the top and bottom ribbons face left.

step 1

2. To make a "sandwich," glue the mate board to the first board, which will act like a cover as it will have no ribbon across it.

3. Flip it over. The middle ribbon now faces left and the top and bottom ribbons face right.

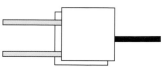

4. Wrap the middle ribbon over the top of the board to face right again.

step 2

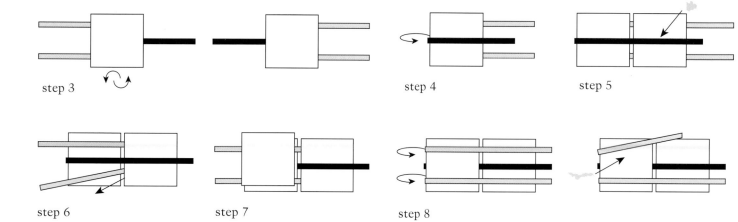

step 3 step 4 step 5

step 6 step 7 step 8

5. Glue the middle ribbon to the bottom board from the second set (the right-hand board, in this case).

6. Pull the top and bottom ribbons out from under. Face them left.

7. Place the other piece of the second set wrong-side-up (if there is a wrapped, unpainted, or wrong side) on top of the two ribbons on the left.

8. Wrap the top and bottom ribbons (by folding over to the right) and glue down to the **left** board only. This is the back of that second board.

9. Pull the top and bottom ribbons through to the back.

10. Glue the halves together; the glued-down ribbons are hidden inside the sandwich.

11. Place the bottom of the third set of boards under the top and bottom ribbons. Glue the top and bottom ribbons down across the board to the right.

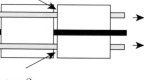

step 9

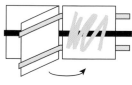

step 10

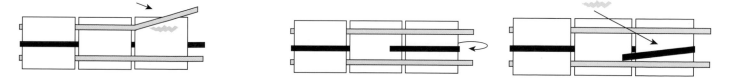

step 11 step 12

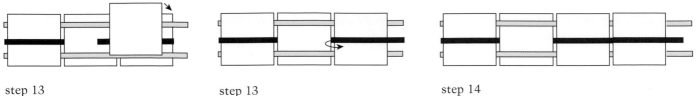

step 13   step 13   step 14

12. Wrap the middle ribbon back to the left. Glue down to the right board.

13. Glue the top of the third set on top of all three ribbons. Wrap the middle ribbon back to the right.

14. Glue the middle ribbon to the bottom board from the fourth set. See step #5.

15–19. For the fourth board, repeat steps 6–10.

20–22. Follow steps 11–13 with the fifth set of boards.

23. Glue down the middle ribbon to the bottom of the sixth board. Trim the end so that the ribbon won't stick out of the last panel, or fold it over to make a hanging loop.

24. Pull out the top and bottom ribbons and face them left.

25. Put the top board of the sixth set on top of the two ribbons on the left.

26. Wrap or fold the ends over and glue them down. Trim them if necessary, so they won't stick out if you don't want a hanging loop.

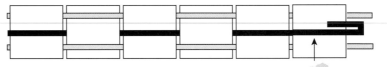

step 23

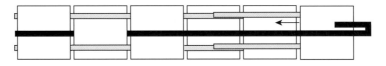

step 24

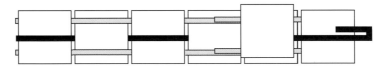

step 25

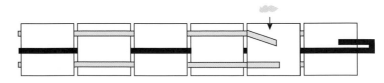

step 26

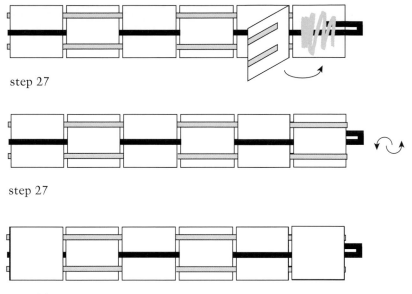

step 27

step 27

step 28

27. Glue the two last boards together with glued ribbons inside the sandwich. This is the "back" or inside.

28. The outside looks like this with no ribbons across the first and sixth panels.

Variation #1: Photocopy close-ups of people's faces to glue over the boards.
Variation #2: Paint the boards.
Variation #3: Use different, decorative papers and wrap the boards first (see "Covering Separate Boards," in Chapter 7).
Variation #4: Use portrait-oriented boards and paper strips one-third the height of the boards less 1/8" in place of ribbons. Align the top and bottom paper strips with the top and bottom edges of the boards.

Uses: toy, hidden text that gets revealed when the book flips over, book about ladders or climbing, intricate party invitation or keepsake, baby book of photocopies of small photographs, anniversary book

Soft and Hard Covers

Cover possibilities vary from simple folded paper to intricate covered boards with spine pieces. When choosing a type of cover, think about the message you wish to convey. A soft cover is less formal, but is appropriate for a single-signature pamphlet or a book with few pages; and it gives some spring to an accordion-folded book. Hard covers protect the book and any delicate pages inside; they weight the paper, helping to keep the book closed, and give a formal appearance.

For some structures, you can paint boards instead of covering them with paper.

During a class at the Oakland homeless shelter, one woman painted the boards for her book blue, then, when they dried, painted them blue again. Then, when I didn't get back to her in time to glue her booklet together quickly, she began to paint them peach. Finally, she said she was too tired. She had wanted to make an address book. She had wanted to make a "real" book. I think she meant a hardcover book with lots of white paper inside.

Working with Glue

When you apply a large amount of glue or paste to cover paper, you must work rapidly. You must also spread the glue evenly. Dip your brush in the glue, then begin in the center of the paper. Work from the center to the

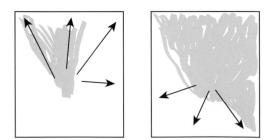

outer edges in a fanlike manner. If you need to add glue, you may dip your brush back into the glue container. Go back to the center and spread more glue outward until all the paper is covered with a thin layer of adhesive.

Soft Wrap Cover
(scoring and folding)

The cover for *Fair Entry* (aka *the cow book*) is a piece of paper heavier than the text paper, folded in half. Beth Herrick and Heather MacDuffie of Port and Starboard Press custom-made the "cowhide" paper.

Fair Entry, 1990, letterpress, collage, single signature, 4³/₄ x 8¹/₄"

Materials: pencil, ruler, bone folder
The cover paper should be the same height as the book and twice the width of a thin pamphlet. Add the depth of the spine if the book's thickness requires this. For a 4 x 6" book with a ¹/₈" spine, the cover should be 6 x 8¹/₈", grained short.

1. Mark, score, and fold the width of the book from each edge with the bone folder (4", in this example).
2. The spine should be in the middle (¹/₈" here).

Uses: Sew this cover with the book block. Glue or tape (with linen tape only) the book block to the fore edges. Glue the front and back covers completely to the book block. Use for single- and multiple-signature books or glue over a stab book bound with thread.

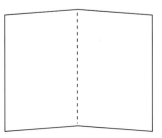

thin pamphlet

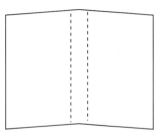

thicker book

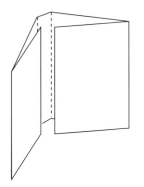

Variation: Use a longer piece of paper, four times the width of the book block plus the spine (if needed). Fold flaps for the front and back covers to add stability to the soft cover. Wrap the cover around the first and last pages of the book or glue the flaps to the endsheets.

variation

Open Spine Soft Cover
(folding)

Diane Meltzer brought me to teach a group of Albany schoolteachers. I taught the simple accordion structure and showed them Talking Alphabet. One teacher looked at the accordion and said, "Now what?" so I showed them how to make an open spine cover and a wrapped hard cover. I have received the same reaction a few times: It isn't complete without a cover.

Materials: bone folder, PVA, glue brush, scrap paper, waxed paper
Two cover papers should each be twice the width of the book block.

1. Fold cover papers in half.
2. Open one cover, and put a flat line of glue along the open edges of the cover.
3. Sandwich the first page of the book; fold at the fore edge. The open part will be along the spine. Smooth down. Put waxed paper between the cover and the rest of the book block.
4. Repeat for the back cover and last sheet.

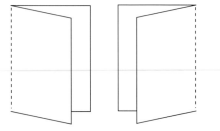

step 1

If you use an open-spine soft cover for the pocket book, you lose a pocket, front and back. If your cover paper is slightly thin, you may want to trim most of each pocket (only first and last). Unfold; use your knife to cut along the bottom fold, up until 1/2" from the first vertical fold. Cut vertically to slice off the pocket, leaving just a very short flap.

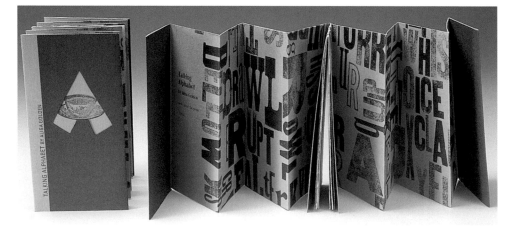

Talking Alphabet, 1994, letterpress, simple accordion, $3^3/8$ x $6^1/4$" (photo by Sibila Savage)

Open Spine with Ribbon
(folding, slitting, gluing)

Do the following if you wish to have a ribbon tie in the back cover:

1. Measure halfway up the fold of the last page and mark. Cut a small slit just a little wider than your ribbon, in the fold.

2. Make a corresponding slit, measuring the same way on the fold of the cover.

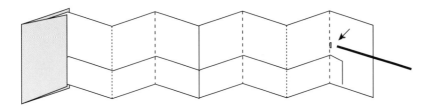 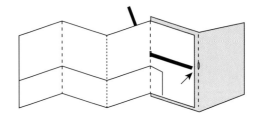

step 1   step 2

3. Thread one long piece of ribbon through the two slits so the ends stick out evenly. The ribbon should show on the back page with the ends disappearing out the back.

4. With a dot of glue, glue the ribbon in place across the sheet. When you glue the covers, put glue on half the cover at a time.

5. Open the cover. Spread glue in a fanlike manner to completely cover half the cover.

6. Smooth down onto the first page.

7. Do the second half in the same manner. Glue the other cover. With the last page, leave the ribbon threaded through the accordion and the cover as you do this.

8. Apply glue to the inner part of the cover; press down over the back page and the ribbon.

9. Turn the page to the back. Open the back cover, apply glue, then press down to the back of the last page.

10. Insert waxed paper between the cover and the next page, front and back.

11. Put waxed paper on top and under the book; then, put the book under weights overnight.

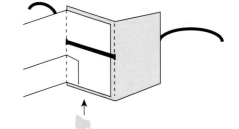

steps 3 and 4

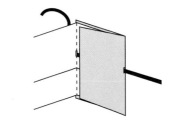

complete

Uses: accordion-fold book, star book, any book that has an exposed or flexible spine

I created handmade paper envelopes from abaca sheets to tuck into the pocket book. Abaca sheets are made from concentrated, processed inner

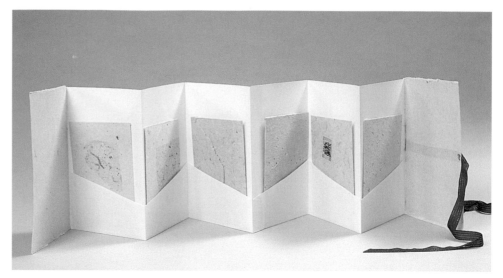

Pocket book with handmade paper envelopes, 1995, 5¹/₂ x 8³/₄"

bark from a kind of banana tree and can be purchased at some art supply and papermaking supply stores. You can also use cotton linters. Abaca and linters are both like very dense paper. To use, soak the sheet in water, tear it into small pieces, and pulp the pieces in a food processor.

Wrapped Hard Cover
(folding and tucking in)

This is a simple, non-adhesive way to attach a hard cover. I used this cover for *My House I Sweep Out*.

Materials: bone folder

Example: 4¹/₄ x 5¹/₂" cover

Paper: two museum boards, 4¹/₄ x 5¹/₂" (2- or 4-ply); two cover papers, 4¹/₄ x 7¹/₂", grained short; two cover papers, 5¹/₂ x 6¹/₄", grained short (can be different color from first)

step 1

steps 2 and 3   step 5

1. Fold one inch in on the top and bottom of the long pieces.
2. Fold one inch in on the sides of the short pieces.
3. Take one board and wrap one of the shorter, fatter pieces around it.
4. Turn the wrapped board over.
5. Tuck the sides of the long thin piece into the first paper.
6. Repeat for the second board.

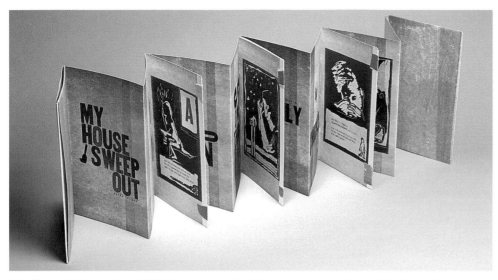

My House I Sweep Out, 1989, letterpress, linoleum cuts, accordion with tabs and signature combination binding, 6¹/₈ x 10¹/₈"

7. Take one end of the book and tuck it into the cover. Repeat for the other end to the second board.

8. If a spine is desired, cut a piece of paper 2 x 5¹/₂", grained long.

9. Measure the depth of the book, and mark the spine piece, leaving an equal distance on each side to tuck.

10. Score with the bone folder.

11. Tuck into the wrapped boards.

step 7

Uses: This style cover works with signature books, flutter books, accordions, and most other books as well.

Hard Covers

When you are ready to do a series of hard covers at home, go to a lumberyard (or similar place), and have them cut up a piece of double-sided smooth Masonite into 12 x 16" boards. The boards can be any thickness, but heavier is better. Each time you glue a book or cover, place waxed paper between the part you glued and the rest of the book block so that the dry pages won't warp. Cover the entire book with waxed paper, and sandwich it between the boards. Place a heavy weight, dictionary, or art history book on top. Press overnight or for several days, depending on the amount and type of adhesive used, size of the book, and temperature and humidity of the room. If you use PVA glue on a hot, dry day, you may not need to press the book at all. A book made with paste only on a cold, rainy day may require a week or more under weights.

Cut 4-ply museum board with a heavy-duty utility or mat knife (not a lightweight, small, pointed-edged knife) against a metal ruler. You will get a better cut by standing up and leaning your weight onto the ruler and the knife. Keep fingers away from the edge of the ruler. Always use a sharp blade. If you make a ragged edge, smooth it out with very fine sandpaper.

Many of the adhesive hard covers require that you leave a $3/16"$ gap between the board or boards and the spine to enable the book to hinge open. If you consistently use 4-ply boards, buy a couple of $3/16"$ spacing bars, available at hardware stores, which will make it easier to place the boards parallel and will ensure the correct spacing. If you use heavy cover paper or thicker boards, you will need to create a gap wider than $3/16"$. Vicky Lee told me about spacing bars after Mary Laird showed them to her. Mary Laird is the proprietor of Quelquefois Press, in Berkeley, California, and she paints, makes books and prints, and teaches letterpress and book art classes.

Measure and cut a spine, if needed, after the signatures are all sewn. Cut the cover paper $1/2–1"$ larger than the signatures on all sides.

Traditionally, glue is applied to the entire cover paper; then the boards are glued, the corners cut, and the flaps turned in immediately. I find it easier and less sticky to apply glue as I go, adding it sparingly each time I adhere a flap.

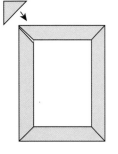

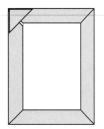

covering a mistake

Covering a Mistake

When gluing hard covers, the board will peek out if you cut the corner of the covering paper too close to the edge of the board. The best technique is to allow the width of the board plus the paper before cutting, but if you make a mistake, you can salvage the project: make a patch by gluing the cut corner over the gap, then glue the endsheet on top.

Insetting a Title

If you want to glue a title to the front cover, you may apply PVA to the back of the title strip and glue it down, or you may prepare your cover boards with a slight well or inset. If you create an inset, the title will lie flush or slightly lower than the boards, which will make it less likely for the title strip to pull up or fall off.

To prepare a front cover for an inset: Use two 2-ply boards for the front cover, one 4-ply board for the back cover, and one spine piece, if applicable. Make sure all the boards are the same size with the grain going the same way (preferably parallel to the spine).

1. Measure and cut a hole from the center slightly larger than the title paper you will be gluing down.

2. Using mostly PVA in a paste mixture, apply glue to the back of the 2-ply board in which you just cut a window.

3. Immediately turn the board over and laminate (a fancy word for glue down) the window board to the remaining uncut 2-ply board. Wrap this in waxed paper and put it under a weight to dry, or continue to make your hard cover and put it under a weight when the boards are all covered.

Backing Cloth

While you can buy paper-backed cloth to cover books and boxes, you will have more variety and freedom of choice if you purchase cloth from a fabric store and back it with paper yourself. The paper gives the cloth added strength, prevents the adhesives from leaking through, and stops the boards from showing through. The cloth has a certain quality that, to some people, feels professional and therefore "real." My feeling is that cloth and paper are appropriate at different times for different books. Cloth is, in general, a little more difficult to work with and shows spots of glue readily. Paper is more forgiving. When you work with cloth, use straight wheat paste with no PVA added at all, to avoid shiny, non-removable glue spots on your book. It is helpful to keep a damp rag nearby for wiping your fingers.

Tips: Light- to medium-weight cotton works nicely. My students all want to use silk right away. Use silk only after you have practiced many times with cotton. It is expensive, and glue or paste will easily stain it. Cloth grain should match the grain of your boards. Test it by stretching the cloth first one way, then the other. If it bows, you are stretching it against the grain; if it seems taut, you are stretching it along the grain.

Use a piece of thin but not sheer mulberry paper or *Yatsuo* or other non-distinguishably grained Asian paper, the same size or slightly larger than the piece of cloth you are backing. Do not use cloth larger than the paper because the ends have a tendency to unravel.

If you will be covering boards immediately, you will not need to let the cloth dry before proceeding. If you will be covering boards at a different time, place the cloth between sheets of waxed paper and dry flat overnight under a heavy weight.

Materials: wheat paste mixed to a creamy but not runny consistency; glue brush; scrap paper; spray bottle of distilled or clean water; waxed paper; smooth surface or tabletop that can get damp; bone folder; cloth; light-weight soft paper cut slightly larger than the cloth (mulberry paper works very well)

1. Iron your cloth if necessary.
2. Spread the cloth flat on the table, face- or good-side down.
3. Mist it lightly, smoothing it down with your hand. Make sure it is not too wet and doesn't have big wet spots. Let it dry a little if it does.
4. Spread out magazines nearby.
5. Apply paste from the middle outward, in a fanlike manner, to the back of the paper. Make sure the coat of paste is even and free of lumps. Pick out the lumps if you find any.
6. Carefully pick up the sticky paper and turn it over, aligning or centering it on the cloth.
7. Smooth it down and let dry.
8. Trim the paper to the cloth when dry, if you like.

To cover boards: Proceed as when using paper, except use only a slightly thicker version of the paste mixture you used to back the cloth. A light, even coating is preferred. Do not use any PVA.

Variation: Have a color photograph made into a (reversed) color transfer (some copy shops with color copy machines will do this); iron it onto the cloth before or after the cover is glued. Set your iron on the highest heat and surround with clean paper, the edges of the cloth not being imprinted. Put the cloth face-up; put the transfer face-down. Hold the iron down on the back of the paper for 10 seconds, then quickly peel it off. You must peel straight and not diagonally or the image will be distorted. More transfer techniques are described in Marjorie Croner's book *Fabric Photos.* (If, as Croner does in her book, you use black-and-white photocopies, make sure they are fresh ones. I tried photocopies that I had had from 1983, and they didn't transfer.)

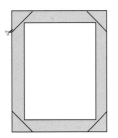

step 3

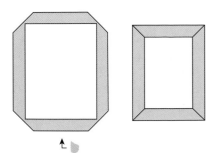

step 5

Covering Separate Boards
(cutting, gluing)

For a retelling of the biblical story of the binding of Isaac, I used an accordion structure attached to separate boards. I added a ribbon that has to be wound around the book to keep it closed. Many readers dislike having to figure out how to wind it.

Materials: waxed paper, bone folder, glue and brush, scrap paper, pencil and ruler, scissors

1. Place the cover sheet, wrong-side-up, on a piece of scrap paper. Apply glue in a fanlike manner, from the center out, spreading evenly.

2. Center one of the boards on the glued sheet.
3. Cut diagonals at the corners, leaving a slight margin. (Don't cut right up to the edge of the board.) Remove the triangles.

The Binding, 1986, letterpress, linoleum cuts, accordion, 4³/₄ x 7¹/₈" (photo by Saul Schumsky)

4. Move the work to a clean surface; discard the scrap paper.

5. Glue, fold, and rub down the side flaps over the boards.

6. Place one endsheet wrong-side-up on a second piece of scrap paper. Apply glue completely to all edges.

7. Pick up carefully and center this paper on the covered board. Press and rub down.

8. Repeat for the second board.

9. Place the covers between two pieces of waxed paper and put between Masonite boards. Put books or bricks on top. Let the covers press flat at least overnight, preferably for a couple of days.

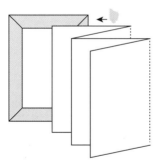

steps 6 and 7

You can also paint the boards instead of wrapping them in paper. Attach them to your book block by putting glue on the back and pressing to the endsheets.

In one class I taught at the homeless shelter, a man painted his boards with water, then did a watercolorlike wash. On top of this he painted trees and black dots on his boards. He asked for a straw, and when we couldn't find one, rolled up a piece of paper and tried blowing at the dots.

"Can I make a birthday card instead?" he asked. He didn't want the inner paper to sew, so he just glued the boards to one piece of stiffer folded paper. When all was put together, he painted "Happy Birthday" on the front. It was clear he had had previous training in lettering. He used two colors of ribbon to tie it, and made a beautiful card.

Uses: accordion-fold book, pocket book, Jacob's ladder, exposed stitch

Split Board
(gluing)

Glue the cloth spine between the double boards (see the standing model), or wrap it around the top and bottom of the outer set of boards like a portfolio (the purple model).

Materials: knife, cutting mat, ruler, pencil, PVA glue, glue brush, scrap paper, waxed paper

Example: $5^3/_4$ x $4^1/_2$" cover

Paper: one spine piece of book cloth cut to $2^1/_2$ x $7^1/_2$"; one paper spine piece cut to $2^1/_2$ x $5^1/_2$", grained long; four 2-ply boards, $5^3/_4$ x $4^1/_2$", grained long

First, sew a book block as for the Exposed Stitch without the French knots, substituting a spine piece (cut the same height as your book and approximately 2" plus the depth of the book) for the full cover paper.

To glue:
  1. Cover your workspace with old magazines. Apply glue to the wrong side of the book cloth.
  2. Glue down one inch of the top and bottom of the book cloth to itself, leaving two folded edges.

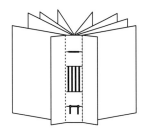

book block

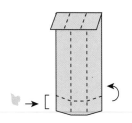

step 2

Split board binding, blank books, 1995

3. Apply a little glue to the pieces you just folded down, up to within ¹/₈" from the top and bottom.

4. Wrap around the book block, gluing the cloth and paper spine pieces together. Smooth down.

5. Open the book block. Brush a thin layer of glue to the edge of the back inner paper spine. Align one board and press down. Repeat for the front inner paper spine. Put waxed paper inside between the boards and the book block. Close the book.

6. Put a thin, even layer of glue on the second board. Align the board (connected to the book block) to the first board, pressing firmly and rubbing down. Repeat for the other side. Wrap in waxed paper and press under a heavy book overnight.

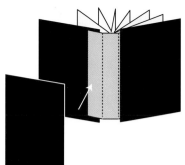

steps 5 and 6

Variation #1: Cover your boards with decorative paper first.
Variation #2: Paint one side of each of the boards with acrylic paints first.
Variation #3: Leave out the cloth spine; sew as for Exposed Stitch with the French knots.

Uses: journal, guest book, sketch book

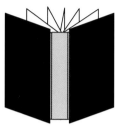

complete

Hard Cover: Side-Bound
(cutting, gluing)

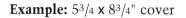

I dreamed a complete story about a hungry family living in wartime and about finding an altar with food on it. The point of the story turned out to be that although the woman who put it there perceived herself to be very religious, she was selfish and stingy. She clearly did not practice her religion in the spirit it was meant to be practiced. The dream became the book *Buddha's Bowl*; it had an Asian feel, so I chose the Japanese side-bound book and the colors red, gold, and black. I included a quote from the Buddha.

Make the cover several days before you need the book, to allow time for it to dry because you must sew the text block to the cover. Punch holes with a leather punch or an awl after the cover is dry, otherwise the cover paper will tear.

Materials: ³/₁₆" spacing bars, waxed paper, bone folder, glue and brush, scrap paper, pencil and ruler, scissors

Example: 5³/₄ x 8³/₄" cover

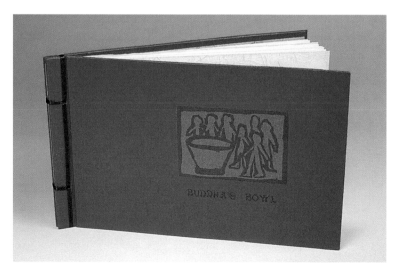

Buddha's Bowl, 1993, letterpress, linoleum cuts, side-bound, 8 x 5"

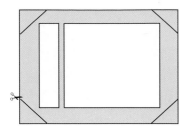

steps 3, 4, and 5

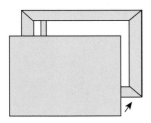
step 7

Paper: two 5³/4 x 8¹/2" museum boards, grained short; two cover sheets, 8 x 11", grained short or with no grain; two endsheets, 5¹/2 x 8¹/2"

1. Cut 1" off of each board so you have four pieces: two 1 x 5³/4 (front and back spines) and two 5³/4 x 7¹/2".
2. Place the cover sheet, wrong-side-up, on a piece of scrap paper. Apply glue in a fanlike manner.
3. Place one of the 1" strips down approximately ³/4" from the 8³/4" edge of the cover sheet.
4. Leave approximately ³/16" (You can put a ³/16" spacing bar here as a guide; take it out before wrapping the boards), and place one of the 5³/4 x 7¹/2" boards lined up with the strip.
5. Cut diagonals at the corners, leaving a slight margin. (Don't cut right up to the edge of the board.) Remove the triangles.
6. Fold and rub down the sides over the boards. Move to a clean surface.
7. Place the endsheet wrong-side-up on a second piece of scrap paper. Apply glue completely to all the edges.
8. Pick up carefully and center this paper on the covered boards. Press and rub down.
9. Repeat for the second board.
10. Place covers between two pieces of waxed paper and put these between Masonite boards. Put the books or bricks on top. Let the covers press flat at least overnight, preferably for a few days.

Variation: Punch holes in the boards and use screwposts instead of sewing.

Photo album with gold ribbon, 1995, side-bound, 8¹/2 x 4⁷/8"

Hard Cover: Single Signature
(cutting, gluing)

When adding a hard cover to a single signature, be aware that the book may not open completely. A single signature was all I needed for my book *Shadowinglovenote*. The story is about a man and woman who need each other to interpret the world around them. I used photocopies of pictures of Europe that Michael took when he was a kid.

Tips: On all sides, cut cover paper ¹/₂–1" larger than the signatures. You may wish to draw light pencil lines on the inside of your paper to line up the boards. These lines will not show.

Materials: paste/glue mixture, glue brush, scrap paper, waxed paper, bone folder, pencil, ruler, scissors

Example: For a 4¹/₂ x 5³/₄" book, the cover should be 6¹/₂ x 7³/₄", grained short

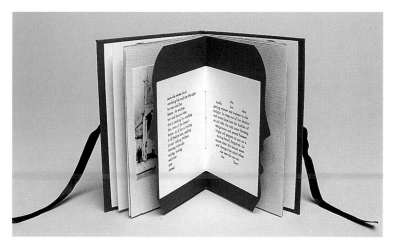

Shadowinglovenote, 1990, letterpress, photocopies (of 1960's photographs by Michael Budiansky), single signature, 3³/₈ x 4³/₄"

  1. Spread magazines over your work surface.
  2. Find the center of the cover paper and mark it with pencil, or fold.
  3. Apply glue to the back of the cover paper, in a fanlike motion, covering one half the paper.
  4. When half the paper is covered, apply one board to the exposed glue, leaving the border (¹/₂–1") that you chose. Press down.
  5. Apply glue to the other half of the paper.
  6. Leaving a margin for the spine, place the other board on the glued paper and press down.
  7. Cut diagonals across the corners, leaving the paper the width of the board before you cut.
  8. Glue and fold down the edges, one at a time, in any order.
  9. Remove the project to a clean work surface. With waxed paper between the bone folder and the paper, rub down the glued paper.
10. Get new scrap paper. Open the first page of the signature and put it on top of the scrap paper, leaving the rest of the signature closed. Apply glue evenly in a fanlike manner only to the back of this paper.
11. Pick up and arrange this page on the front board with the margins you chose.
12. Rub down with the bone folder. Put a piece of waxed paper between the newly glued sheet and the rest of the signature. Close the book and face it to the left.
13. Open the back cover. The rest of the signature should be closed on the left.

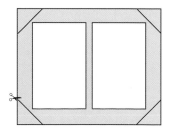

steps 4, 6, and 7

14. Put a piece of scrap paper between the last sheet and the signature. Apply glue to the back of the last sheet. Remove the scrap paper.

15. You may need to close the book slightly (possibly to a 45-degree angle) to obtain the same margins as the front inner cover. Press down onto the back board.

16. Over waxed paper, rub down with the bone folder.

17. Place waxed paper between the newly glued sheet and the rest of the signature. Close the book.

18. Place between Masonite boards. Put a heavy weight on top. Let dry overnight.

Hard Cover: Multiple Signature
(cutting, gluing)

This hard cover adds a spine to the basic single-signature cover.

Tips: To find the width of the spine needed, put one board atop your book block, and measure from the table up to the last signature.

Materials: paste/glue mixture, glue brush, scrap paper, waxed paper, bone folder, pencil, ruler, scissors

Example: For a $4^1/4$ x $5^1/2$" book with a $^3/8$" spine, the cover paper should be 10 x $6^1/2$", grained short.

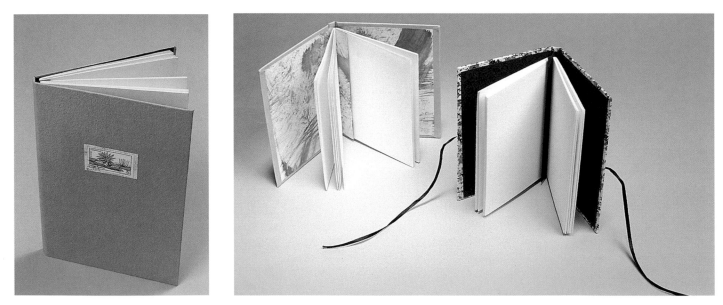

Left: Lavender blank book with postage stamp, 1995, two-sewn-as-one, 6 x $9^1/8$"
Right: Two-sewn-as-one models, purple with ribbon, 1995, 4 x 6 x $^3/8$" spine, orange with acrylic ink endsheets, 1996, $4^1/2$ x $5^1/2$ x $^1/4$" spine

1. Spread magazines over your work surface.
2. Put the cover paper wrong-side-up. Find the center on the back of the cover paper and mark it with a pencil, or fold.
3. Apply glue to the center of the cover paper; glue down the spine.
4. With a fanlike motion, apply glue to cover one half the cover paper.
5. Put a spacing bar next to the spine. The bar will probably be on top of some exposed glue; that's okay. Abut the board. Remove the spacing bar.
6. Apply glue to the other half of the paper.
7. Put down a spacing bar, then the board; remove the bar, and press down the board.
8. Cut diagonals across all the corners, leaving the paper the width of the board before you cut it.
9. Glue and fold down the edges, one at a time, in any order.
10. Remove the project to a clean work surface. With waxed paper between the bone folder and the paper, rub down the glued paper.
11. Continue as for the single signature, steps 9–17.

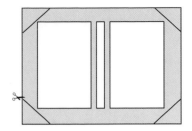

step 8

Hard Cover: With Ribbon
(gluing)

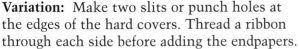

Once your boards are covered on the outside, proceed as follows:

1. Center a ribbon, roughly 24" long or twice the width of your boards plus at least 12", in the middle of the back board or the board that will be the last. Center both vertically and horizontally.
2. Put a dab of PVA glue to hold it down so it will stay there when you paste down the endsheet or end accordion.
3. Continue as for gluing a signature or accordion book. See page 117, steps 9–17 or page 113, steps 7–9.

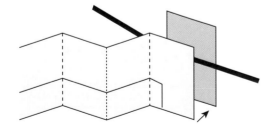

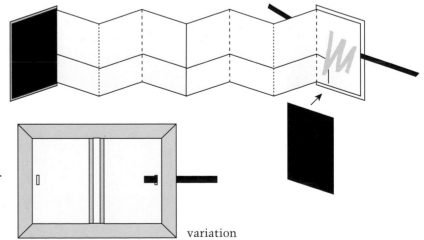

variation

Variation: Make two slits or punch holes at the edges of the hard covers. Thread a ribbon through each side before adding the endpapers.

Hard Cover: Accordion/Signature Combination or Hinged Cover
(cutting, gluing)

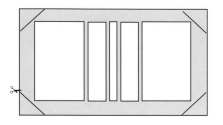

You will use five boards: front and back covers (the width of the signatures), spine, and two pieces the height of the book but the width of the accordion.

Follow the directions for a hard cover for a multiple signature, adding the two extra pieces, the width of the accordion, between the spine and the front and back covers, with a $^3/_{16}$" gap between all the boards. Attach the accordion to the covers, aligned with the boards; then, paste down the endsheets on top.

Hard Cover: Ribbons at Spine
(cutting, gluing, slitting when dry)

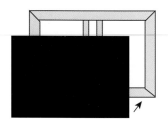

step 1

Follow the directions for a hard cover for a multiple signature; then, add an endsheet in place of the book block.

1. Put glue on the single long piece of paper that will serve as the endpaper.

2. Arrange on the front board (you should have an even $^1/_8$–$^1/_4$" border all around); rub down with a bone folder.

3. Leave the covers, sandwiched between waxed paper, under weights at this time. Let dry for 2–7 days, depending on the size of the book and the humidity.

Left: *Paper Has a Memory*, 1995, rubber stamps, solar prints, typewritten pages, unique, 6 x 5$^1/_2$", and accordion/signature combination, 1995, Canson Mi Teintes paper, 5$^5/_8$ x 5$^1/_2$"
Right: Multiple signature onto ribbon, 1995, blank books, peach ribbons: 4$^5/_8$ x 5$^3/_4$ x $^3/_8$" spine, yellow ribbon: 4$^1/_2$ x 5$^1/_2$ x $^3/_4$" spine

CHAPTER 8

Portfolios and Boxes

A Note on Boxmaking

Boxes can be containers for a series of loose pages or cards, or they can be protection for a book. In general, if a book has a hard cover, it does not need a box, although it may look nicer in one. A box or slipcase can protect a thick softcover book. It can present two or more related books together or make a hardcover book look more formal.

A portfolio functions best when it houses loose pages that can be viewed coherently in any order. If the pages are numbered, the reader has to do additional work to make sure the story is in order. Poems or non-sequential prints or photographs work well in a portfolio.

If you have a set of prints, photographs, or loose pages, the box serves as a frame as well as protection. Choose cover materials to reflect or enhance the contents.

A Note on Closures

Some boxes and books require a tie or link so they do not spring open. A paper strip glued in a loop is fine for a temporary closure, but it is not practical for permanent use. You can use paper, ribbons, bone closures, buttons, Velcro, or other boxes to secure the book.

I have stopped using ribbons, except for hardcover portfolios, because I have found that readers often worry that they will be unable to tie the ribbon again "correctly." By providing a smooth transition from the outside to the inside you will tempt the reader to open your book. If the closure is too fussy, the would-be reader may be discouraged or intimidated.

Four in Transport, 1989–1990, four books in a shaped two-piece box, 6 x 10"

The extra time it takes to open a book or box sometimes adds suspense and contributes to the feel of the book. Bone closures add dignity to books and boxes; if you use two, point the ends toward each other. Velcro works for the sturdy postcard portfolio, but for added durability you will need to sew it down in addition to gluing it. Buttons and string can provide a range of interesting closures, depending on the type. To make your own buttons, use a polymer clay, such as Sculpey or Fimo, bake it hard in the oven, then varnish it for a custom look. When you choose a closure for your book or box, think about the message you wish to convey as well as the function.

Folded Envelope

Time: 5–10 minutes

I used this envelope style as covers in the set of three books titled *Catching a River*. I adapted it for a cover, after Anne Schwartzburg mailed me a flyer folded up this way.

Materials: ruler, pencil, bone folder

Paper: rectangular, any size
  1. Put paper in front of you horizontally (landscape orientation).
  2. From the top left corner, measure 2" down and 2" to the right. Mark with a pencil.
  3. Repeat for the other corners.

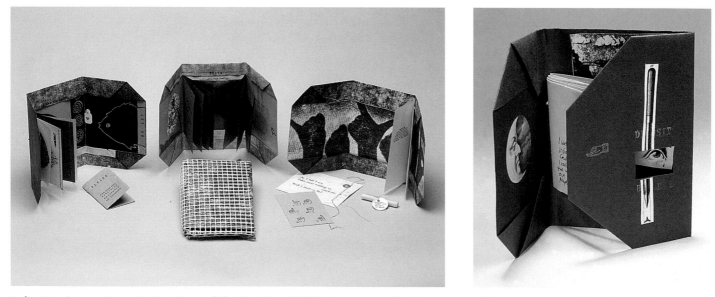

Left:: *Catching a River: Delta, Dreamfish, The Island,* 1993, letterpress, linoleum cuts, rubber stamps, mixed media, envelope covers, 4¹/₈ x 6¹/₈"
Right: *Jury Rig,* 1992, mixed media, envelope model, 3¹/₂ x 5"

4. Fold up the corner so it touches the pencil mark.

5. Repeat for all four corners.

6. Bring up the bottom edge and fold it over 1", aligning the edge with the bottom two pencil marks, making an even, straight line.

7. Repeat for the top edge.

8. From the left and right, fold the paper into thirds. Tuck one flap into the other and crease down.

Variation: Sew a single signature into the fold.

Uses: book cover, self-folding letter, prospectus for a book

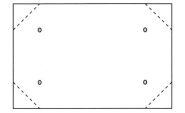

steps 1 and 5

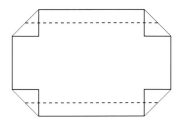

step 6

Pocket Folder

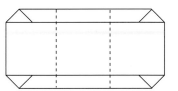

step 8

Time: 20–40 minutes

This looks like the school folders you can buy in the grocery or stationery store, but it is surprisingly handsome when you use thicker, handmade paper. I made my first pocket folder when I was sending sample photographs to the publisher of this book and didn't want to send the pictures in an ugly, plain folder.

Materials: pencil, ruler, knife and cutting mat, PVA, glue brush, scrap paper, waxed paper, 1" coin or other small, heavy circle

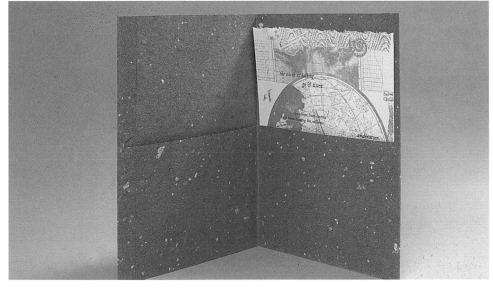

Pocket folder with *Earthwords* broadside, 1997, 9 x 12"

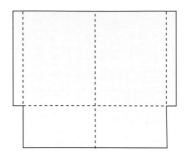

steps 1–4

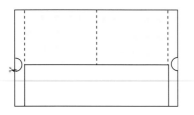

step 5

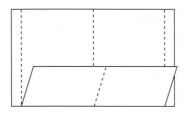

steps 8, 9, and 10

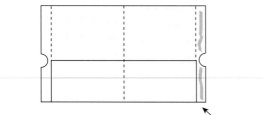

step 11

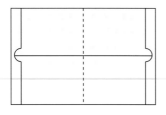

complete

Paper: 20 x 17", grained short, to make a 9 x 12" folder with a 5" pocket

1. Put the paper in front of you horizontally (landscape format).
2. Measure 1" from the right and left edges. Score.
3. Measure 5" up from the bottom. Score.
4. From the bottom edge, cut vertically along two of the outermost score lines to leave two 1 x 12" flaps at the right and left edges.
5. Fold up the bottom flap.
6. Score and fold the folder in half.
7. Fold over the edge flaps. They will be glued on top of the pocket.
8. Trace around the coin or circle with a pencil, drawing a half-circle, centered, where the pocket will end.
9. Repeat for the other side.
10. Cut out the half-circles, rounding the edges.
11. Open the side flaps; apply a thin, flat line of glue; and press down.
12. Wrap in waxed paper. Press overnight under weights.

Paper Portfolio
(folding, gluing and sewing on a button)

Time: 25–55 minutes

Val gave me a paper portfolio many years ago that is still useful for carrying books. Michael and I examined it closely. He made a pattern for me; then, I made my own.

I like making simple buttons of polymer clay for the portfolio. I flatten and shape the clay, poke holes with a toothpick, and bake it in my preheated toaster-oven on low heat for about a minute. The toaster-oven gets really hot and the clay can char at the edges if you don't watch carefully. Let the button cool before handling it.

Materials: needle, one button, macramé cord, knife, cutting mat, bone folder, PVA glue, small glue brush, scrap paper, ruler, pencil

Paper portfolios with clay buttons, 1997, red with jute, Larroque Mouchette paper: 16 x 10", white with raffia, Indian wool paper: 5³/4 x 4³/4"

Paper: heavy paper, such as St. Armand, Somerset, Lenox 100, Rives BFK, Canson Mi Teintes, or Indian Village

Example: This example makes a small envelope. Use paper 16 x 23", grained long, to make a 9 x 12" portfolio. You will still use the same side measurements in the following directions. Measure up from the bottom to 9" instead of 4¹/2".

1. With the cover side down, if one side of your paper is different from the other, turn your paper vertically (portrait orientation). Measure 2" from right and left sides.

2. Mark and score with the bone folder. Do not cut. Fold in.

3. Measure in from the folded edge at 1". Mark and score.

4. Fold the edge back to the place you just scored, making an accordion fold. You should have two edges, each with two folds at 1" and 2".

5. Measure up from the bottom, 4¹/2". Mark, score, and fold. Unfold.

6. Measure 2" from this fold; mark, score, and fold.

7. Measure 4¹/2" from here; mark, score, and fold. You should have 3" remaining at the top. Unfold.

8. Now you will make one opposite fold by turning the paper over. When you turn it over, the two valley folds will become peak folds. Match the two folds, dividing the 2" space into two 1" spaces, with a valley in the middle.

9. Open completely.

10. With your knife, cut one slit on each side of the 2" squares.

11. Take the corner of each tab and match it to its opposite corner, folding a triangle. Do the other corner this way. Repeat with the other square. You have just folded an "X".

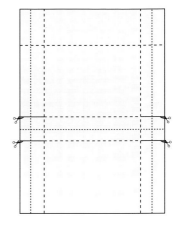

steps 9 and 10

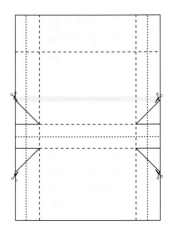

step 12

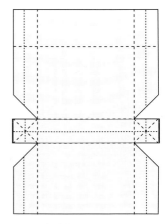

steps 1–13

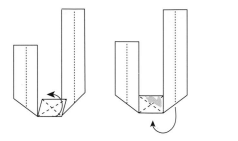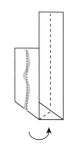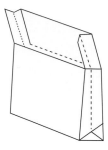

steps 14 and 15 steps 15 and 16 steps 18 and 19

12. With your knife, cut a diagonal on each side of the squares as follows: measure 1" from the square on each side. Draw or cut directly a diagonal line from the inside corner of the square to the mark you just measured.

13. Repeat for the three remaining sides. Put aside these triangular scraps.

14. Glue up as follows: with a tiny brush or your fingers, put glue on the side edge of the folded "X", along that side's triangle on the back. (See the diagram.)

15. Bring up one long side (the side with the 3" flap at the top) and align the cut with the "X". Repeat for the other long edge.

16. To glue the remaining whole sides, put glue along all the edges, overlap, aligning to the "X", and press into place.

17. Repeat for the other short side.

18. Recrease the now-glued folds.

19. Fold the 3" side over the top.

20. Sew a button onto the outside of the envelope, centered and about $1/2$" from the edge flap. For durability, you may want to first glue down one of those scrap triangles underneath.

21. Poke a hole on the bottom pocket, thread macramé cord through it, and tie off. Glue a scrap triangle to the back to cover the knot and enhance its strength.

Uses: portfolio for transporting books, stationery holder, stack of cards

Hardcover Boxes and Portfolios

Many of the techniques for making hardcover books are applicable to making boxes. These techniques include using light-weight to medium-weight paper or backed cloth, and cutting corners or insetting a title. Cut the cover paper $1/2$–1" larger than the intended box size on all sides, to allow for the gaps between the boards. The inner papers should be $1/8$–$1/4$" smaller on all sides. The proportions for the hardcover boxes and portfolios (with the exception of the slipcases) assume you use 4-ply museum board, which is 1/16" thick.

PVA glue is essential to building boxes with rigid walls as it is strong and dries quickly. Use paste or a paste/glue mixture when covering the boards; this will give you a little time to reposition the boards before the glue sets.

The time required for each project depends upon the size and complexity of the box. Larger boxes or ones with many pieces take more time; allow yourself a few hours to make and cover them.

Painted Slipcase
(scoring, folding, gluing)

Time: 10–15 minutes to paint, 10–15 minutes to build

I went with Lisa Kokin to teach at the Oakland homeless shelter. I taught one book structure and this slipcase. One man painted the boards for the book with solid-gold acrylic paint. Then he painted "God love you" in red. Several of the students pointed out that "love" should have had an "s" on the end. But he liked it the way it was. He painted the box black with red and gold dots and began to make a series of cuts in the slipcase board, unlike my example. Then, he asked for needle and thread. Sewing his box together, he tied it up and presented the bundle to Lisa. He had made the project his own and was happy.

The following example is only cut and glued. Paint the inside a bright, contrasting color.

Two slipcases, 1995, left: painted, 5 x 6 x 3/4", right: papered

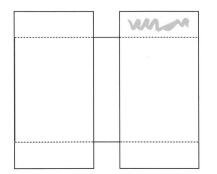

step 4

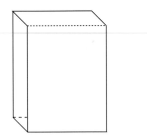

complete

Tips: Prevent ragged folds by scoring the museum board first with your knife. Bend the flaps against the score or place your ruler next to the score and bend up against the ruler.

Materials: knife, bone folder, cutting mat, ruler, pencil, scrap paper, stencil brush for painting, acrylic paints, gel medium (optional), PVA glue

Example: 6" tall x 5" wide x 1½" deep open box (slipcase)

Paper: one 2-ply board cut to 11½ x 9", grained short

First, quickly paint the fronts and backs of your two boards, using acrylic paints straight from the tube or squeezed out onto a paper towel with no added water. Keep the paint thin and dry, not gloppy. Paint the edges as well. The boards should dry within a couple of minutes.

1. Put your 2-ply board horizontally in front of you. Measure 1½" from the top and bottom of the board. Mark and score lightly with your knife against the side of the ruler. You should have two horizontal lines.

2. Measure 5" from the left and right edges of the board on what will be the outside of the slipcase. Mark and score (a light cut with your knife) two vertical lines. The distance between the two lines should be approximately 1½".

3. With your knife, cut out that 1½" square in the center top and center bottom of your board. Crease and fold up all other edges.

4. Apply PVA glue to one flat edge of one of the top flaps. Pull the other flap over it and press together. Hold for five to ten seconds while the glue sets. Repeat for the bottom flaps, gluing the opposite edge under instead of over. One flap from the right side should be under one from the left, and one flap from the left should be under one from the right.

Uses: protection for several softcover books, box for a book with painted covers

Covered Slipcase
(scoring, folding, gluing)

Time: 25–35 minutes

Ear. Egg. Yam. Coconut. has a version of this covered slipcase with a letterpress printed covering sheet. The title of the little books comes from a quirky desire to use things that had different colors inside and outside.

Materials: knife, bone folder, cutting mat, ruler, pencil, scrap paper, glue brush, scissors, PVA glue, wheat paste, gummed reinforcement tape or self-adhesive linen tape

Ear. Egg. Yam. Coconut. 1987, slipcase, 3¹/₄ x 4¹/₄", with four bookettes, 3 x 4"

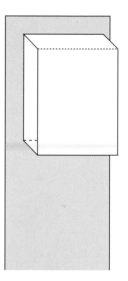

steps 3 and 5

Example: 6" tall x 5" wide x 1¹/₂" deep covered, open box

Paper: one piece of 6 x 16" cover paper or book cloth, grained long; one back spine piece, 1³/₈ x 5⁷/₈", grained long; one 2-ply board cut to 11¹/₂ x 9", grained short

1. Build the box as for the Painted Slipcase.
2. Cut two squares of gummed reinforcement tape or adhesive linen tape and place over the two short, open slits made by the back flaps at the spine.

Your box is ready to be covered with a glue/paste mixture, not straight PVA glue.

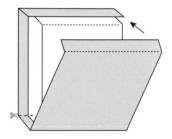

step 6

3. Put down magazines for scrap paper. Put the long cover paper on the scrap paper, wrong-side-up, oriented vertically.
4. Apply paste to the entire top half of the paper.
5. Place the box ¹/₂" from the top edge of the paper and centered side to side.
6. Apply the glue/paste mixture to the last section, rubbing down and rolling the box over so you can work around it. (You may choose to apply glue to the whole piece of paper, but I find it unwieldy working with so much exposed glue.)
7. When the box is wrapped, cut slits at each corner. These slits will allow you to wrap the paper over the front edges and inside the slipcase.

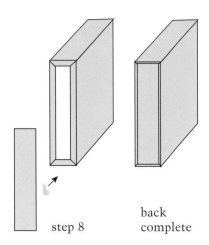

step 8   back complete

For the back you may wish to cut straight slits, then taper them by cutting slight diagonals. Glue, and rub down. For the front (open end), just glue and fold over inside the box. Rub down.

8. Apply PVA or the glue/paste mixture to the back spine piece. Place over the back of the box. Rub down.

Uses: protection for several softcover books or one hardcover book, stand for the piano hinge book

Hardcover Portfolio with Ribbon Tie

This is an improved version of the first portfolio I made in 1983, *the world is sick she cried, so let's dance*; it has a folded-over spine that leaves no gaps at the head and tail. I remember making wheat paste from regular, food-grade flour. The portfolio still looks the way it did when I made it, although the outer Canson Mi Teintes paper has faded a little. You can get more information about making portfolios from *Creative Bookbinding,* by Pauline Johnson, and from *Books, Boxes, and Portfolios,* by Franz Zeier.

Materials: scissors, pencil, ruler, glue/paste, glue brush, bone folder, scrap paper, waxed paper, awl, cardboard to protect work surface

Left: *the world is sick she cried, so let's dance* (portfolio of linoleum cut prints), 1983, letterpress, linoleum cuts, 12¹/₄ x 16¹/₈"
Right: *the world is sick she cried, so let's dance* (interior)

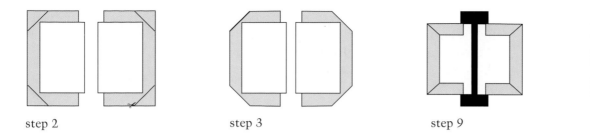

step 2   step 3   step 9

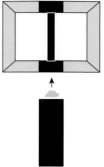

steps 10 and 11

Example: $9^1/_2$ x 12" portfolio

Paper (all grained long): two 4-ply museum boards, $9^1/_2$ x 12"; two pieces of decorative paper, $9^1/_2$ x 14"; two light-weight inside sheets, 9 x $11^1/_2$"; one piece of heavier or contrasting paper or book cloth, 4 x 12"; one yard of ribbon; one light-weight piece for the inside spine, 4 x 9"

 1. Apply glue to the back of one sheet of the decorative paper.
 2. Place the museum board on top so that one inch of board remains uncovered.
 3. Cut diagonals on the two corners. Remove the two corners (triangles).
 4. Fold down the edges over the boards. Use a bone folder to rub down.
 5. Repeat for the other board.
 6. Place the outer spine, wrong-side-up, vertically in front of you.
 7. Measure $1^1/_2$" from the right and left edges; draw a line with a pencil.
 8. Apply glue to the strip of outer spine paper or book cloth.
 9. Place the two boards on the pencil line. Press down.
10. Fold the spine paper over the top and bottom of the boards and press down.
11. Apply glue to the back of the inner spine paper. On the inside of the portfolio, align the sides of the inner spine with the outer spine, making sure it is centered at the top and bottom. Press down.

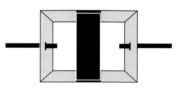

steps 11 and 14

To add ribbons, continue below, or skip to step #17:

12. Cut two pieces of ribbon, one for each board.
13. Measure $1/_2$" in and halfway down the boards.
14. Poke a hole in each board with an awl or wood gouge, or cut a slit as shown.
15. Thread the ribbon through, leaving $1/_2$–1" of ribbon inside the cover.
16. Apply a little glue to each ribbon. Glue down to the boards.
17. Apply glue to the back of the inside paper. Place down on one board, being careful that the ribbon is lying flat.
18. Put waxed paper on the board and rub down with a bone folder.
19. Repeat for the other board.
20. Place waxed paper to cover the Masonite board. Place the portfolio on the waxed paper, open. Cover with waxed paper and another board. Put weights on top.

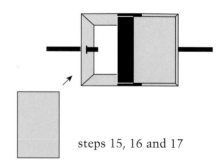

steps 14 and 15

steps 15, 16 and 17

Note: If you make a larger portfolio, you can put the waxed paper inside and press with the portfolio closed.

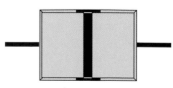

complete

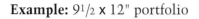
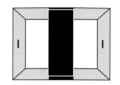

Hardcover Portfolio with Envelope Pocket

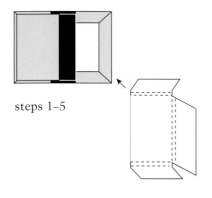

steps 1–5

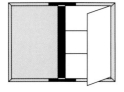

complete

For this structure you will make the hardcover portfolio without ribbons but with a right-hand pocket in place of the inner paper. This is like *A Tea Party*.

For a 9 x 11^1/$_2$" envelope with 4^1/$_2$" flaps top and bottom, 8^1/$_2$" flap on the right side, and ^{1}/$_4$" deep, you need a medium– to heavy-weight paper, 17^3/$_4$ x 20^3/$_4$".

Do steps #1–11 of Hardcover Portfolio.

1. Place the paper in front of you vertically.

2. From the right, measure and mark at 8^1/$_2$" and 8^3/$_4$". Score two lines.

3. From top and bottom measure up/down 4^1/$_2$" and 4^3/$_4$". Score these four lines.

4. Cut out the rectangles at the corners along the inner score (rectangles will measure 8^3/$_4$ x 4^3/$_4$").

5. Valley fold along all score lines.

6. Proceed with steps #17–20 of Hardcover Portfolio. Use the paper you just prepared instead of the right-hand inside paper.

Left: *A Tea Party* (portfolio of color linoleum cut prints), 1993, 11 x 15"
Right: *A Tea Party* (interior)

Postcard Portfolio

Carry this with you on your travels, to protect picture postcards, carry stamps, and have an instant hard surface for writing.

Materials: knife, cutting mat, metal ruler, pencil, glue brush, chisel tool, two bone closures, scrap paper, PVA glue, wheat paste, scissors, 3/16" spacing bars, Velcro (self-stick or sew-on) and/or button and string, thread, needle

Example: $4^1/_2$ x $6^1/_2$ x $^1/_4$–$^1/_2$" portfolio

Nine pieces of board: *front and back,* two $4^1/_2$ x $6^1/_2$", grained long; ***for the left middle spine,*** one $^3/_8$ x $6^1/_2$; grained long; ***for the right middle spine,*** one $^1/_2$ x $6^1/_2$", grained long; ***for the side flap,*** one 2 x $6^1/_2$", grained long; ***for the top and bottom flaps,*** two $4^3/_8$ x 2", grained short; ***for the top and bottom spines,*** two $^1/_4$ x $4^3/_8$", grained short

Six cover papers: one book cloth, $7^1/_2$ x $13^1/_2$", grained short; two book cloths, $3^1/_2$ x $5^3/_8$", ***top and bottom flap covers,*** grained short; ***one inner paper,*** $6^3/_8$ x $12^1/_8$", grained short; ***two inner flap papers,*** $4^1/_8$ x 3", grained short

1. Arrange the boards in front of you from left to right: one front board, the $^1/_2$" middle spine, back board, the $^3/_8$" middle spine, the right flap.

2. Spread out scrap paper and put out cover paper or book cloth horizontally (landscape), wrong-side-up.

3. Measure a $^1/_2$" border; draw a line in pencil for a guide.

4. Apply paste/glue in a fanlike manner (from the middle to the edges) to the left third of the paper, up to the pencil guide.

5. Press down one cover board.

6. Put the $^3/_{16}$" spacing bar next to the board and abut the $^1/_2$" inner spine; press down. Remove the spacing bar.

7. Apply glue to the rest of the paper inside the $^1/_2$" margin.

8. Glue the other cover board, use the spacing bar, then glue the $^3/_8$" spine, use the spacing bar, then glue down the right flap.

9. Turn over and smooth down with a bone folder over waxed paper.

10. Turn back over. Cut off the corners with scissors, leaving the width of the board plus the paper (at least $^1/_8$").

Postcard portfolio, 1995

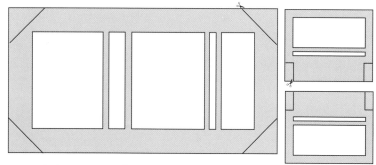

steps 1, 2, 10, 13, and 17

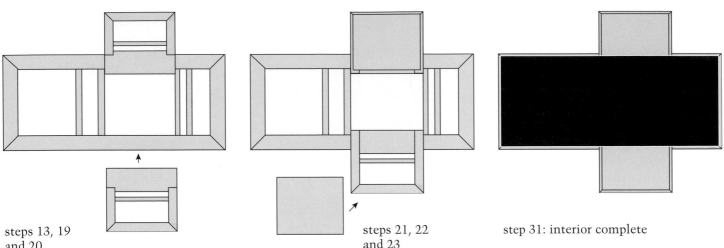

steps 13, 19
and 20

steps 21, 22
and 23

step 31: interior complete

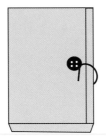

complete

11. Spread glue on each of the cover flaps and turn them in, one by one. After gluing two flaps, get fresh scrap paper and continue working.

12. Set the covered boards aside while you prepare the top and bottom flaps.

13. Put one of the $3^1/2$ x $5^3/8$" flap covers wrong-side-up, in front of you vertically on top of scrap paper.

14. Measure a $1/2$" border around the right, left, and top sides, and draw a line in pencil for a guide.

15. Apply glue.

16. Align one flap board, then a spacing bar, then a $1/4$" strip. Remove the spacing bar.

17. Cut two corners at the top. Glue and fold over the left, right, and top edges. Rub down.

18. Turn the flap over. Put glue on the bottom $3/8$" on the right side of the book cloth or cover paper.

19. Center and press down to the row of boards you glued previously on the right-hand cover board. You should have a margin between the flap spine and the big board.

20. Repeat steps #13–19 and attach the bottom flap.

21. Use new scrap paper; spread PVA glue across the back of one of the inner flap papers. Paste is not sticky enough for this step.

22. Center and rub down on the flap.

23. Repeat for the other flap.

24. Attach button/string now or skip to step #31.

25. Measure halfway up the far-left cover board (when the inside is showing), and $3/4$–1" in; mark with a pencil.

26. With a narrow awl, poke holes that correspond to the holes in the button.

27. Sew on the button, making several loops through the button and the cover to secure it. Tie off in a square knot.

28. On the right cover (not the spine or flap), make a corresponding hole $1/2$" from the right edge of the cover. (You will have the spine and right flap on your right.)

29. Knot approximately one foot of cord or thin ribbon. Thread from the inside to the outside.

30. Take a dot of straight PVA and glue down the knotted cord as well as the threads from the button.

31. Apply glue to the final inner paper, center on the previously glued boards, and press down. The paper will cover the ends of the inner flap papers and the button/string stitches (if applicable).

Variation: Use self-adhesive Velcro in place of button/string. Stick on after the portfolio is completely covered. Then sew a decorative button or beads to the front cover, through the Velcro, with thread the same color as the Velcro. The sewing reinforces the Velcro (self-stick will pull off with repeated opening and closing).

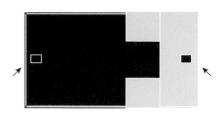

Variation

Two-Piece Box
(gluing)

Make one box with edges flush, another box with a lipped edge. Val and I had an art day where I showed her how to make this box. Since we had been exchanging so much mail art, we made boxes to hold each other's letters. She likes umbrellas. I glued extra boards underneath in an umbrella

Two-piece box to hold letters from Val, 1989

shape, much the same way you would inset a title, then wrapped the box with glued-down paper.

Materials: glue brush, scissors, scrap paper, bone folder, waxed paper, knife, pencil, ruler, cutting mat or pieces of cardboard to protect the work surface, paper plate for paste or glue, gummed or self-adhesive linen reinforcement tape, $3/4$–1" wide; four pieces square for corners, glue/wheat paste combination, PVA to glue boards together

Example: $8^3/4$ x $5^1/2$" box

Fourteen pieces of paper: *for the front and back,* two large boards $8^3/4$ x $5^1/2$", grained long; *for the four top and bottom ends,* two trimmed to $5^7/16$ x $1^1/2$" and two to $5^1/4$ x $1^1/2$"; *for the four side pieces,* two $8^3/4$ x $1^1/2$"; *for the cover,* two light-weight pieces of book cloth or paper for the outside, $16^1/8$ x 13", grained long; *for the inner paper,* two decorative or light-weight black paper rectangles, $8^1/2$ x $5^1/4$"

1. Arrange these sets of board pieces side by side as follows: a large board (vertical), short side pieces top and bottom, long side pieces right and left.
2. Trim the side pieces. The left-hand box (lid) will have two long pieces the length of the cover board, and two end pieces $1/8$" less than the width. The right-hand box (lipped bottom) will have a long piece $3/8$" less than the length of the cover board and two end pieces $1/2$" less.
3. On the large, right-hand board, measure $3/16$" around all the edges. Draw lines with your pencil. This will be the bottom of your box, the "lipped" side.
4. With a small brush, apply straight PVA glue to the edge of one long side piece of the right-hand board and stand it up along the line, perpendicular to the large board. Hold it a minute or so until set.
5. Apply glue to one short side, putting a little on the edge that will touch the side you just glued down as well.
6. Repeat for the third and fourth sides.
7. For the left part of the box (the top lid), glue in a similar manner, this time lining up the pieces on top of the board at the very edges. Check that the sides are not hanging over. Put away the PVA.
(In the following steps I use the word "glue" or "paste" for the paste/glue mixture only.)
8. Place a square of linen or paper tape to join the side pieces inside each of the four corners for reinforcement.
9. Place the book cloth or paper, wrong-side-up, on your work surface. Center the box, open-end-up.
10. With a pencil, draw around the edges.
11. Repeat for the other box.
12. Remove the box parts.
13. Apply the paste/glue mixture to the place where the base of the box will go. Affix the box.
14. With a ruler and pencil, extend the lines so they look like a tic-tac-toe grid.

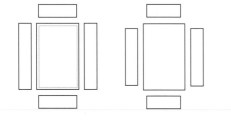

steps 1, 2 and 3

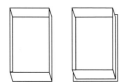

steps 4, 5, 6 and 7

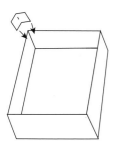

step 8

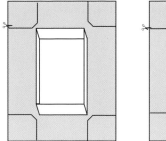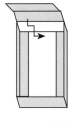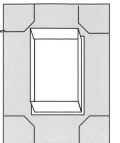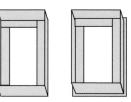

steps 15 and 16

steps 17, 18, 19 and 20

step 20

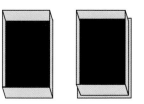

steps 22 and 23 complete

15. Draw diagonals across the corners. Leave at least $1/4$" between the box and the corners you will cut. (See the diagram.)

16. Cut along the lines and across the corners, making sure the cover paper will overlap slightly to cover the box corners.

17. Apply paste to another edge of the paper to wrap over the side of the box.

18. You may need to trim the edges slightly so that you don't have too much overlap inside.

19. Repeat for all the edges.

20. Smooth into all corners and joints with a bone folder; put waxed paper or other protective sheets between the bone folder and the box.

21. Check that the lining papers will fit into the box without running up the inner walls. Adjust by trimming, if necessary.

22. Apply glue to the back of the lining paper. Smooth into place.

23. Repeat for the other side.

24. Line the boxes with waxed paper and put a weight on top. Leave to dry overnight or a few days.

Clamshell or Presentation Box
(gluing)

Materials: glue brush, scissors, $3/16$" spacing bar, scrap paper, bone folder, waxed paper, knife, pencil, ruler, cutting mat or pieces of cardboard to protect the work surface, paper plate for paste or glue, four $3/4$–1" square pieces of gummed or self-adhesive linen reinforcement tape, PVA to glue boards together

Example: $8^3/4$ x $5^3/4$" box

Fifteen pieces of paper: *for the front and back,* two large boards, $8^3/4$ x $5^1/2$", grained long; *for the four top and bottom ends,* two trimmed to $5^7/16$ x $1^1/2$" and two trimmed to $5^1/4$ x $1^1/2$"; *for the two side pieces,* one trimmed to $8^3/4$ x $1^1/2$" and one to $8^9/16$ x $1^1/2$", grained long; *for the spine,*

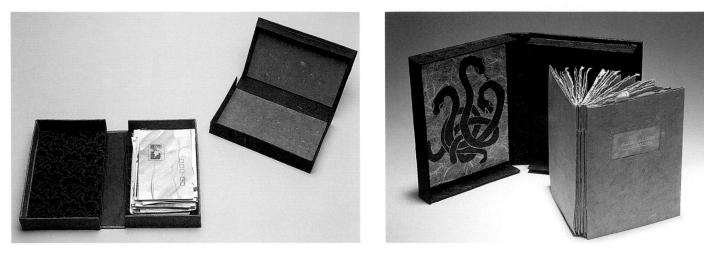

Left: Presentation or clamshell boxes, 1996, 5³/4 x 8³/4 x 1¹/2" deep
Right: *Waking Snakes,* 1996, letterpress, linoleum cuts on paper custom made by Magnolia Editions, slot and tab binding, 3¹/2 x 5" book in 4 x 5¹/2" clamshell box

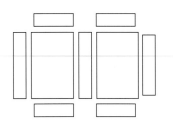

steps 1 and 3

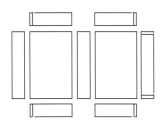

step 2

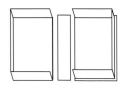

steps 4, 5, and 7

one 8³/4 x 1¹/2", grained long; **for the inner boards,** two 2-ply boards, one trimmed to 5⁵/16 x 8⁷/16" and one to 5¹/16 x 8¹/8", grained long; **for the cover paper,** one light-weight piece of book cloth or paper for the outside, 20 x 15", grained short; **to cover inner spine,** one light-weight piece of book cloth/paper (*Yatsuo* or mulberry is good), 4 x 8⁵/16", grained long; **to cover the 2-ply board,** two thin book cloths, cloth or paper 6¹/4 x 9¹/4", grained long

1. Arrange the boards in front of you as follows: the large board on the left, side pieces on the top and bottom, long side piece on the left, spine in the middle, then large board on the right, side pieces on the top and bottom, long side piece to the right.

2. Trim the boards to the above specifications. The left-hand box (lid) will have a long piece the length of the cover board, and two end pieces ¹/16" less than the width. The right-hand box (lipped bottom) will have a long piece ³/8" less than the length of the cover board, and the two end pieces ¹/4" less.

3. On the large, right-hand board, measure ³/16" around the edges: top, right, and bottom. Draw a line with your pencil. This will be the bottom of your box, the "lipped" side.

4. With a small brush, apply straight PVA glue to the edge of one (top or bottom) side piece, stand it up along the line, perpendicular to and aligned with the left edge of the large board. Hold it a minute or so until set.

5. Apply glue to the long side piece, putting a little glue on the edge that will touch the side you just glued down as well.

6. Repeat for the third side.

7. For the left part of the box (the top lid), glue in a similar manner, this time lining up the pieces with the very edges of the board. Check that the sides are not hanging over. Put away the PVA.

In the following paragraphs I use the word "glue" or "paste" for the paste/glue mixture only.

8. Place a square of linen or paper tape to join the side pieces inside each of the four corners for reinforcement.

9. Place book cloth or paper, wrong-side-up, on your work surface. Find the middle of the paper. Put the spine here.

10. Measure $3/16$"(or use a brass bar for a spacer) from it on the right, and put down the "lipped" part of the box.

11. Measure $3/16$" from the left, and put down the top of the box.

12. With a pencil, draw around the edges.

13. Remove the box parts.

14. Apply the paste/glue mixture to the place where the spine will go. Affix the spine.

15. Apply the paste evenly, in a fanlike manner to the right; affix the lipped box bottom.

16. Repeat for the top of the box.

17. With a ruler and pencil, extend the lines so they look like a tic-tac-toe grid.

18. Draw diagonals across the corners. Leave at least $1/4$" between the box and the corners you will cut. (See the diagram.)

19. Cut along the lines, making diagonal slits on either side of the paper that will cover the spine.

20. Apply paste to one long side of the paper that is cut diagonally near the spine; bring up and press, wrapping the triangular piece around the exposed side of the board.

21. Before you press the rest of the paper down over the top, trim the edges of the paper to make a flap the same size as the box edge. Press into place.

22. You may need to trim the edges slightly to avoid too much overlap in the corners. Repeat for all the edges.

23. Smooth into all the corners and joints with a bone folder, preferably rubbing with waxed paper or other protective sheets between the folder and the box.

24. Check if the inner spine lining will fit into the box over the spine without bending at the top and bottom. Adjust by trimming, if necessary.

25. Apply glue to the back of the inner spine lining paper. Press into place, smoothing into the joints.

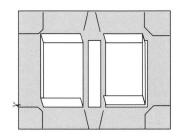

step 9

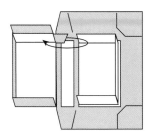

steps 18 and 19

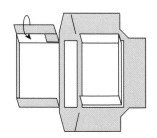

steps 20 and 21

step 21

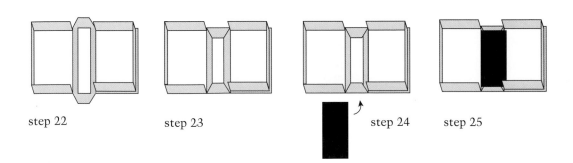

step 22   step 23   step 24   step 25

Now, for the last two covered boards that will be the final lining:

26. Make sure these covered boards fit into your box, the larger one on the left, the smaller one on the right.

27. Turn the inner cloth/paper wrong-side-up. Apply paste over the whole sheet, center the 2-ply board, and rub down.

28. Cut diagonals at the corners. Glue down the flaps.

29. Repeat for the second board.

30. Make sure the larger board goes on the left, and the smaller board goes into the "lipped" side. Put glue (paste/glue or PVA) on the uncovered/partly covered side all the way to the edges; turn over and glue into the box.

31. Press down firmly.

32. Repeat for the other side.

33. Line the box with waxed paper, and put a weight on top of the waxed paper inside the box. Leave to dry overnight or a few days.

steps 27, 28
and 29

step 30

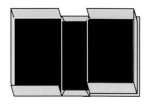

complete

step 32

CHAPTER 9

Easy Ways of Decorating Paper

By adding a decoration or title strip to your book you can distinguish the front cover from the back. I am constantly frustrated by handmade books that are completely blank on the outside, that do not signal which side I should open. Create a small collage, rubber-stamp or stencil a title, or paint some paper and cut it into a title strip. Inset the art for a finished look (see "Insetting a Title," in Chapter 7). These methods can also be used to decorate endsheets, soft covers, or paper portfolios.

Small Collage for Cover
(cutting and gluing)

Via Hand book, 1990, collage, letterpress-lined, two-sewn-as-one, 5 1/8 x 6"

Time: 10–30 minutes

Materials: knife, extra blades, cutting mat, glue and small brush or glue stick, miscellaneous images, metal ruler, decorative-edge scissors

A few quick tips:

  1. Start by cutting loosely or tearing out of their backgrounds three or more images that appeal to you (pick a theme if this makes the choices easier). Move them around a little, see if certain ones go together better than others (you don't have to use everything you like). Pick out the ones that work together, and use your knife to cut around the edges.
  2. Make sure you have extra blades for your knife. Images look best when cut precisely to their edges.

Four blank books, 1995, collage, single signature, lavender bookettes: $4^1/_2$ x $5^1/_2$", black bookettes: $4^3/_8$ x $7^1/_2$"

3. Use a combination of cut and torn edges; you may like the look of wavy-edged or zigzag scissors as well.

4. Use added light and dark papers for contrasting backgrounds.

5. Experiment with textures/patterns.

Stenciling
(cutting, painting)

Time: 5–30 minutes

For a very simple stencil, purchase a decorative punch from a stationery or art supply store; designs available include flowers, hearts, cows, fish, musical notes, cats, etc. Punch into a medium-weight paper and use the cutout for your stencil. Paint over it onto other paper using acrylics and your stencil brush. Alphabets of different sizes are available at office supply stores and art stores.

To make your own stencil:

Materials: knife, cutting mat, metal ruler, simple one- or two-color design on plain paper, waxed stencil paper or Dura-lene (a Mylar drafting film with a matte finish that feels like a cross between plastic and paper. Don't use acetate; it will tear.)

1. Mark three X's on the edges of your design: two on the top at each corner, one at the bottom in the middle. These will be your registration marks.

2. Place the stencil paper on top of your design and trace it, including the X's.

3. If you have a second color, place a second sheet of stencil paper on top of your original design (otherwise known as "key-line drawing") and trace it, also including the X's.

4. Cut out carefully with your knife.

5. Rub the back of the X's with the side of your pencil. Center your design on your page, lightest color first. Before you apply paint, draw on top of the X's with a sharp pencil or pen, transferring them to your page. With a small, flat-bottomed stencil brush, dip into acrylic paint (you can use it straight from the tube), and apply it evenly in each area you cut out. Let it dry.

6. For each color, repeat with other stencils. You should be able to line it up by looking through the stencil paper or by lining up each set of X's with the faint pencil mark on the page.

OH, 1996, stencil, book of household ephemera, collage, chain stitch, $4^1/_4$ x $5^1/_2$"

Carving Rubber Stamps

Time: 5–15 minutes per image

One Thanksgiving I sat and listened to Michael, his dad, and his step-grandfather all talk about a hat and Russia. The conversation bordered on the absurd and made me laugh, so I wrote it out. I printed it and it became the book *HAT. Hat. hat.* I carved and printed erasers for the images of well-bundled Russians, metaphorically depicting Michael's grandmother's story of her family.

I also cut rubber stamps out of erasers to print the pictures for *Paper Wings*. I made a butterfly and a labyrinth. Each sheet of paper is cut in half, length-wise, with a different text at the top and bottom. You can mix and match the two stories: one of a butterfly that doesn't want to emerge, the other of Icarus' fictitious daughter.

With enough time, you can make a whole alphabet just from erasers.

Materials: white plastic erasers, knife, linoleum-cutting tools, fine-point permanent marking pen or small photocopies, pencil, nail polish remover (if you wish to remove the printing from the eraser before beginning or if you are using photocopies), cotton balls for the nail polish remover

Note: With linoleum-cutting tools, always cut away from you, and keep your fingers behind the tool.

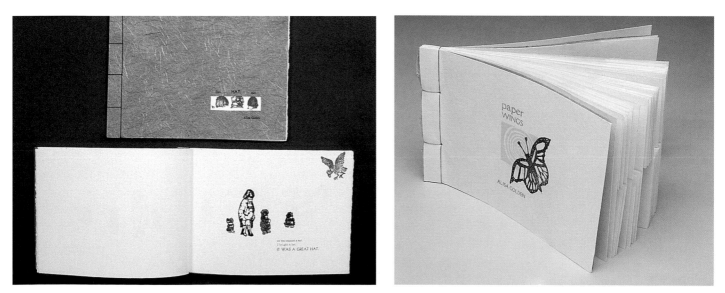

Left: *HAT. Hat. hat.*, 1989, letterpress, hand-carved rubber stamps, side-bound, 10 x 7"
Right: *Paper Wings*, 1992, letterpress, hand-carved rubber stamps, side-bound, 4 x 6$^{1}/_{2}$"

For a hand-drawn image:
1. Cut the eraser to the size you desire.
2. Draw your design (backwards from how you wish it to look) on the eraser.
3. Draw over your design with the permanent pen.
4. With your knife, cut around all the edges as if you were drawing, but don't cut away any of the eraser yet.
5. Cut away any part you don't want to print, using the linoleum-cutting tools or your knife.

Using photocopies (photocopy your design if you don't feel comfortable attempting to draw backwards):
1. Choose a small image or letter that will fit on your eraser.
2. Cut it out with a border you can hold on to.
3. Place it, image-side-down, on your eraser.
4. With a cotton ball soaked in nail polish remover, rub the back of the photocopy, carefully holding the photocopy in place.
5. Check periodically to see if the image is transferring.
6. When the image looks clear on the eraser, remove the photocopy and discard it.
7. Proceed by cutting around the image with your knife and cutting away any part (such as white space) you do not wish to print.

Painting with Acrylics

Time: 10–30 minutes, depending on paper size

I learned to loosen up by watching Anne Schwartzburg when we first started painting with inks on 120 large sheets of paper for *Tidal Poems*. We spread out ten pieces of 22 x 30" paper at a time, and then we ran around scribbling circles and randomly scrubbing color into the paper. As a letter-press printer accustomed to examining one piece of metal type at a time, I found it was hard to begin.

Since then, I have found this method of decorating paper particularly satisfying and tension-releasing. I painted big words and sentences for the backs of the pages in *Ezra's Book* and then I painted over the words. My son, Ezra, was born with unexpected complications, and when he was well again I was able to work through the stress by painting.

I made the covers for *Magic* by painting bright colors, waiting for them to dry, then painting black or purple on top and scratching out words in the black paint while it was wet.

Just put paint all over your paper. Use only one color and white, or use two colors that aren't complementary, and it should look great. Complementary colors are those that mix to make brown, such as red/green, yellow/purple, blue/orange. Wear old clothes or a smock: acrylics don't come out once they are dry—and they dry quickly! Mix paint with gesso to make lighter colors that are less shiny and to give a tooth to the surface; this makes it easy to draw on them with pencil.

Tips: For a less sticky feel when dry, apply paint sparingly (rub it into the paper) and use only matte finishes, or use paint mixed with gesso. You can also use acrylic inks applied with a soft brush instead of using acrylic paint.

Materials: acrylic paint, gel medium (matte finish), gesso, plastic lid or palette, stencil brush, white or off-white paper, magazines or paper to cover your work surface

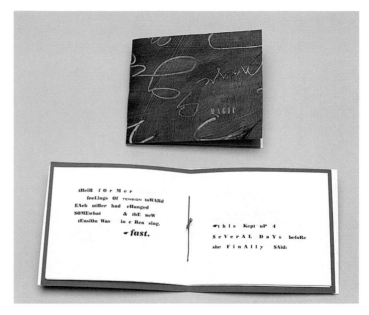

Magic, 1997, photocopy edition, acrylic-painted cover, 4^1/$_2$ x 3^3/$_4$"

1. Use acrylic paints straight from the tube or squeezed out onto a paper towel, palette, or lid, with no added water. Moisten your brush first, and wipe off excess water. Water will weaken your paper and make it curl up and dry more slowly. If the acrylics feel too dry, add gel medium.

2. Keep the paint thin and not gloppy.

3. Brush diagonally, make circular motions, or paint randomly. Cover every bit of white space.

4. Avoid leaving large areas that are just one flat color. Try for a mix of the colors. Brush strokes look nice, too.

5. The paper should dry within a few minutes.

6. When the paper is dry, you may wish to paint on top through a stencil with other colors. If there is a part you really do not like, acrylics are opaque and you can cover that part easily.

Variation #1: Use acrylic inks. Paint large words on a big piece of paper. Let dry. Paint more lines and words on top with other colors. Cut up into pieces.

Variation #2: Use acrylic inks, but while they are still semi-wet, brush a bit of gesso here and there, back and forth over the lines, to alternately cover and reveal the paint.

Variation #3: Drip or splatter paint with acrylic inks.

Portable Books

Thoughts on Content

A woman came into my class with a basket of books she had made in other workshops. She took them out one by one and the other students and I exclaimed at how beautiful and unusual the books were. But she didn't feel satisfied; the books were pretty, but they were all blank. She wanted to put words or images inside but didn't know where to start.

Experiment with words as you would with art materials. Choose a style. Use it in a book. Complete the project. No matter what type of book you make, you will learn more if you finish it. Then make more. Some writing may be appropriate for a large edition, some just for a friend's eyes.

All types of writing are valid and have appropriate venues. When writing, your primary goal is to get thoughts onto paper. Edit and revise only after you are satisfied you have said everything you need to say. You may find that figuring out your conclusion first will make beginning easier. Or just start, and let the conclusion evolve as you write freely. For more inspiration, read Natalie Goldberg's *Wild Mind: Living the Writer's Life,* or a *Life in Hand: Creating the Illuminated Journal,* by Hannah Hinchman.

A book that has a punch line will most likely be discarded or ignored once the punch line is reached. But if the book has many layers, whether physical layers or multiple texts, it is more likely that readers will be intrigued and come back again to see what else they can find.

You may have one text but wish to add layers via images. In a papermaking class at California College of Arts and Crafts, Don Farnsworth talked about using layers when making a paper piece. He suggested that showing only part of something was much more interesting and mysterious than revealing everything at one time. The images in your book don't always have to be literal illustrations of the words.

I am very interested in translucent papers because they are easy to layer. Val Simonetti and I used a translucent cover in our collaboration *RE:Memory,* a book of our dreams about our teacher Betsy Davids. For my sister Nina's 30th birthday I printed a book on translucent glassine paper

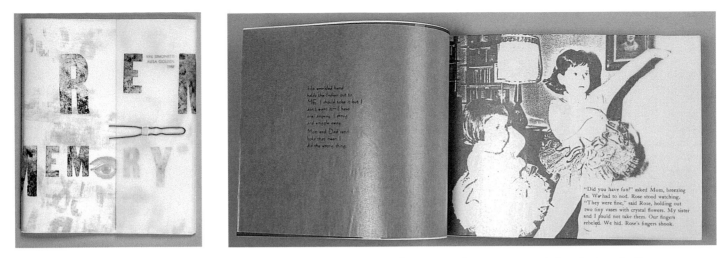

Left: *RE: Memory* (a collaboration with Val Simonetti), 1988, photocopy, letterpress, brayer-printing (a hand-printed offset technique), 5¼ x 7"
Right: *Nina, Rose & me*, 1995, letterpress, photocopy (of photographs by Roger Golden), acetate, wire and beads, side-bound, 6 x 9"

with two texts: one about how we learned to make beaded flowers with an elderly friend, the other about meeting Dr. Shlomo Bardin, and how he gave us a plastic Indian. Dr. Bardin founded the Brandeis Camp Institute (now the Brandeis-Bardin Institute), a Jewish leadership training and educational institute in southern California. In between the sheets, I sandwiched enlarged photographs of Nina and me at different ages, as well as different-colored pieces of acetate. The book *Nina, Rose & me* has layers of text as well as physical layers.

Travel Journal

Where is a good place to start working with layers? Begin with the travel journal.

When you travel, you may start to find yourself lining your pockets with ticket stubs, receipts, stickers, and wrappers. Then, when you get home, you wonder what to do with all this "ephemera." Maybe you don't have to travel past your own neighborhood; you collect ephemera naturally. Create a travel journal or household journal while you are still in transit, or before you have an overwhelming pile on your desk. It is easy to do this every night before bed, while you can still remember little details of the day. I did this when I went to Maine with my family. Betsy Davids made a book with bags she collected in Greece and called it *Excess Baggage*.

You can bind a blank book first if you prefer, but if you compile the loose pages first you can edit or redo the pages before they are permanently attached to one another. I find gluing things or writing in blank books much more intimidating than creating the book one page at a time. It's hard to put that first mark on the paper: I'm afraid I won't like it later.

Creating the pages separately gives you extra time for thinking and repositioning.

If you sort the objects and create the pages before you sew the book, you will have more flexibility. On the other hand, you may find that the travel book you intended to make isn't right for what you acquire. If you can, bring materials for a few different structures.

Bar Harbor Journal: Nine Budianskys, 1996, mixed media, handmade paper for cover by Port & Starboard Press, exposed stitching, 4¹/₂ x 5³/₄"

Starting to Write

You can sort your ephemera and notes in different ways: chronologically, thematically, geographically, or by other category. As you assemble the pages, write small paragraphs or sentences about the objects, in whatever order you wish. Think about what will vividly awaken your memories when you read it again in 20 years.

As you write, don't worry about getting your trip in exactly the right order. Memories backtrack constantly; we tend to remember sequences in pieces, then later add to them. If you have trouble starting, sit quietly for a minute and then write about whichever bit of your journey comes into your head first. See where that writing leads you. You will probably remember something else soon after, and then it will be hard to stop. Just let your hands assemble and write without trying to edit or worry how it will look. You will get more ideas as you keep your hands busy.

Work a little at a time. Experiment. There is no one right way.

Generating Words

The following are some exercises to help you get started.

Automatic Writing
This is a technique that the Surrealists loved and writing teachers often use. Write for five minutes. Don't edit, don't think, don't stop, just write any words that come into your mind. Punctuation is not important. Nothing is important but keeping your hand writing words.

Afterward, look through the words and see if anything interesting jumps out. If you do this as an exercise every day you will eventually find phrases and words that you will want to put in a book. You can find intriguing examples in *The Autobiography of Surrealism: The Documents of 20th Century Art*, edited by Marcel Jean.

Free Association
Pick one word that you like. Write it in the middle of the page. Draw a circle around it. What is the next word that comes into your mind? Draw a

line from the first word and write the second word in another circle. Does this word lead you to another word? Draw a line from it to another circle. If this third word doesn't immediately suggest a fourth word, go back to one of the other words on your page. Keep writing words in this non-linear way until your page is filled. Keep looking around at all the words to think of new ones. Use these words as starting points for a poem or story. Feel free to add other words later. You don't have to be restricted to only the words you generated in this exercise. *Writing the Natural Way: Using Right-Brain Techniques to Release Your Expressive Powers*, by Gabriele Lusser Rico, details how to work with "clustering," a special format for writing out related free-associated words.

Digging a Hole, from *Four in Transport*, 1990, letterpress, linoleum cuts on waxed masa paper, side-bound, 6 x 10"

Found Text

If writing exercises don't inspire you, get out the in-flight magazine and start cutting out words. Spread out the words and arrange and rearrange them. Make a series of sentences. Use a glue stick to put them onto cards or into book form.

Text may also be found in snatches of overheard conversations, or by listening to music with lyrics and writing down the words you like.

Choosing a Title

You can use the place and date as a title or you can seek out a more imaginative name for your travel journal. I keep a list of interesting phrases that could be titles; sometimes one of these fits my current book. In high school I remember reading about a new film by Sylvester Stallone, *Paradise Alley*. I was intrigued by the title, which sticks with me even now. I liked the juxtaposition of "Paradise," which I imagined was light, lacy, and beautiful, and "Alley," which made me think of things earthy, man-made, hard, and harsh. When I was making a book about mothers, pigeons, and homes, I was delighted to find that pigeons were called "rock doves." It reminded me of "Paradise Alley," two dissimilar words. Combining two or more contrasting words has a striking effect.

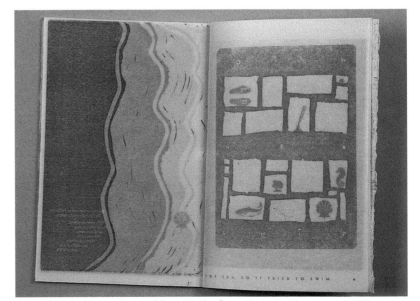

A Feather is Cut to Resemble a Knife, from *Four in Transport*, 1990, letterpress, linoleum cuts on waxed masa paper, side-bound, 6 x 10"

One Knit Heart, One Winter Diamond, 1987, collage, technical pen, unique palm leaf book in a box, approximately 6 x 8" (Photo by Saul Schumsky)

Suggested Materials for a Portable Bookbinding Kit

Pritt glue stick

bookbinding needle, sturdy thread, waxed linen in a few colors

small sharp scissors or folding scissors

binder clip

precut 100% cotton paper (thesis or resumé paper), $8^1/_2$ x 11", cut in half to make $8^1/_2$ x $5^1/_2$", works well for traveling

small stapler and plastic or stainless-steel staples

labels (such as archival labels with a preprinted border)

photo corners

Sakura Pigma micron or brush pens (light-fast, permanent, fine-tip markers or brush markers. These come in many sizes in black and in a set of red, green, blue, purple, black, and brown)

small bone folder

pencil

small ruler

alphabet rubber stamps with pre-inked holder

hole punch

screwposts

bamboo skewers

small art knife with a protective cap

small piece of cardboard on which to cut

sturdy plastic box or container for carrying everything

Suggested Structures for In-Transit Construction

1. side-bound books
2. two-hole around a stick
3. single signature
4. multiple signature with spine strip or soft-wrap cover
5. exposed stitch on soft-wrap cover

6. chain stitch
7. piano hinge on skewers
8. hidden book
9. simple accordion
10. fan
11. palm leaf

Ways of Attaching Collected Ephemera

Pritt glue stick

sewing

stapling

cutting diagonal slits into pages to hold the corners of postcards

photo corners

making pockets in pages

punching holes in objects and the page and tying them together with thread or waxed linen

Printing Text

Getting text or images onto paper may be done in many ways. When you are traveling, handwriting and rubber-stamping your text are the easiest options; they are also the least formal-looking. If you have a laptop computer, you might purchase a portable printer or rent time in a copy shop while on the road. Upon your return, you might letterpress print your story, but that requires lots of skill and equipment. The method you choose may depend more on access to equipment or budget than on your aesthetic preferences.

Using rubber stamps is slightly more formal-looking than handwriting and has a distinctive look. You can achieve this look without spending much money: small alphabets with individual handle-mounted letters are inexpensive. Office supply stores sell sets that enable you to set a whole line or two or three instead of stamping one letter at a time. You can stamp onto most weights and types of paper. Rubber-stamping can be time-consuming if you have a lot of text, however. I like to use the rubber stamps as titles or to emphasize certain words.

Computer-generated type looks the most "real" to some people. Some copy shops have in-house computers that can be rented by the hour. You

When Again Was, 1986, letterpress edition, photocopy, modified side-binding, 4^1/$_2$ x 7"

Three Bags Full, 1993, commissioned by Linda and Bernard Faber, letterpress, single signature, 4¹/₈ x 5"

might find one of these shops while you are traveling. Computers offer a wide range of typefaces. The output is generally clear and can be photo-copied easily. Make a small book about one adventure or a specific place. Attach it to your travel journal or put it in a page with pockets. Structures that require printing on just one or two sides (such as the hidden book or the simple accordion with or without the tunnel) would work well.

Letterpress printing is an involved, relief-printing process that presses metal type into the page. A few old print shops around the world still offer this service. In countries where letterpress is the primary means of print-ing, the cost will be reasonable. Hiring someone to letterpress print a whole book in the United States is costly, but you might want some portion of your trip printed this way: design your own postcard and send it to friends. Keep one in your travel journal. If you will be staying in one place for sev-eral weeks you might look for classes at a book art center to learn how to print your own.

Editioning

When Ed Hutchins came to San Francisco, he bought several copies of dif-ferent picture postcards, cut windows in them, and made them into an edi-tion of tunnel books. You might decide to make an edition of a travel jour-nal this way, too.

An edition is a group of identical, multiple copies of a book that are signed and numbered by the author and artist/illustrator. The numbers

1/40 or 39/40 (number one in an edition of forty, or thirty-nine in an edition of forty) are identifying marks. Some people believe that the lower the number, the better the copy, but this is not necessarily true. I occasionally give my books names instead of numbers, or make them all number one. You may decide to make an edition but change the colors or vary the images as you go along.

While you probably won't collect more than one of each ticket stub or matchbook, you might want to photocopy your pages (color or black and white) and make an edition of your book that way.

About Colophons

After you finish making your travel journal, you can write information on the last page to remind you what materials you used. This paragraph of information is called a colophon. For example, list the kind of paper, the typeface, how the book was printed, how the illustrations were made, the edition number, any credits, and the date. A few years later you may not remember. The colophon helps you identify materials you might like to use again. The colophon is the one place I feel I can loosen up completely. I may add what the weather was like when I made the book, what song I was listening to, or other anecdotes.

General Note

These techniques and writing exercises apply to making any book, not just a travel journal. When I make a book I can begin from many different angles. The shape or style of the structure may remind me of a theme. I may see a paper I want to use and try to think of a reason to use it. A topic may already be in my head (e.g., seeds, relationships, the stars) and I just need to write and then find a structure that relates to the theme. Sometimes I can design a book, choose the structure and the paper, but the writing never comes. At other times I have a poem or story that really doesn't want to be a book. I let it go and move on.

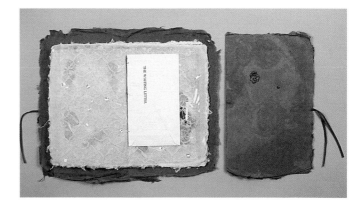

The Waiting Letter, 1985, handmade paper, mixed media, single signature, 6^1/$_2$ x 10^3/$_4$" (photo by Sibila Savage)

Other books you may want to read are *Artists' Books: A Critical Anthology and Sourcebook*, edited by Joan Lyons, and *The Design of Books*, by Adrian Wilson.

Conclusion

 always thought I would have to choose between writing and art; I loved to do both. Only in college did I find that I could merge words and images and make books. I was excited and kept looking at my first book of poems, *never mind the crowd*, over and over, amazed that I had made it. I watched the other students and found they had the same reaction to their books that I had to mine.

Fifteen years after I made my first book, I am still excited when I create a new one. The combination of textures and smells of paper and ink make each book distinct and fresh. I don't think of merging writing and art anymore; I think: "book," and an organic, whole piece evolves. I think about the reader who will interact with my book. I think about how the pace sets a tone: how one page leads to another, briskly, with physical movement, or slowly and thoughtfully. The writing, the art, the paper, and the structure each add a layer to the book to create a mood or clarify a meaning. Sometimes, what I thought I was making turns into something else, something "the book wanted."

The variations are endless. I included in this book only the bindings that, in my view, enhance the final project without appearing overly fussy or complicated.

You may find these bindings elsewhere with other names. Because this form of bookbinding is like a folk art, the bindings have no fixed name. Book artists have a tradition of openly sharing new or better techniques. We see a book, figure out how it was put together, and teach it to others, not always knowing who created it or what it was called. Several of the unusual structures included here were first developed and taught by Hedi Kyle or Keith Smith. This book springs from fifteen years of making books combined with three years of teaching book structures to adults.

Through your mistakes you will find which structures work for you and which can be modified. You can make the same book from many angles; there is no "right" way. Adapt the bindings for your particular project and make them your own. See what your book "wants." Then, pass your findings along to others.

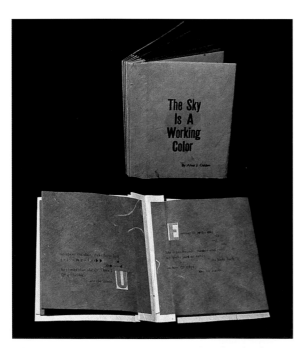

The Sky Is A Working Color, 1985, handmade abaca paper, letterpress, accordion spine with glued pages, $4^{1}/_4$ x $5^{3}/_8$"

Back to front: *Tidal Poems, Lizard's Snake Suit, Waking Snakes, Fly on a Ladder, Cinnamon & Saffron, The Lending Library*

You can make books more exciting to children by giving them a sense of pride as they learn to make their own, or you can make books for children you know that are personal and related to something with which they are familiar. Looking at books in a personal, fresh way can excite and stimulate an interest in reading and writing as well as provide a structure for creative expression.

Book art doesn't have to be mysterious and formal, subject to other people's decisions. You have the power to create your own books. You can present a story in various ways; different book structures enhance each telling. In our expanding world of screens and keyboards, we need handmade books that have texture and smell and a personal feel. If you think you've made a mistake, add to it, change it, and let the book evolve into something else. It's yours.

Appendix

About Paper

Paper Selection

This is my list for those people who work with archival materials. I define archival as materials that are acid-free or pH-neutral to start. Acids are in the air, so unless the book is sealed in a box, unread and untouched by our hands, it will change slightly over time. Buffered papers contain an additive that makes them slightly alkaline to get a head start on the acids. I generally prefer archival materials for making books.

For making books in school, copy paper, manila folders, and white drawing paper are fine. Book art can be created out of anything. You may like the wonderful selection of recycled papers, or you can use various cardboards or paper bags. When doing a photocopy book, I use the 100% rag papers available at the copy store, but they are almost always white.

Here are some suggested archival printmaking/fine art papers for different types of books. (Weights are from the Daniel Smith Catalog.)

Text 95–120 grams/square meter
Books: signature books, slot and tab, chain stitch, multiple-signature books, album/flutterbook, tabs for tunnel books
Suggested papers: Mohawk Superfine, Rives Lightweight, Yatsuo (Moriki), German Ingres, Lana laid, Nideggan, resumé paper, Canson lightweight
Text 160–250 grams/square meter
Books: accordion-fold book
Suggested papers: Lenox 100, Arches, Rives BFK, Canson Mi Teintes, Stonehenge, Somerset Textured/Smooth
Text 40–115 grams/square meter
Books: side-bound book, with pages folded in half
Suggested papers: mulberry paper, hosho, Yatsuo, other Japanese papers, or very light-weight Western papers: Rives lightweight, Lana laid, Nideggan
Text 160–250 grams/square meter
Books: photo album, side-bound book
Suggested papers: Arches black, Fabriano Ingres Cover black, Canson Mi Teintes black, German Etching black, Stonehenge, Lenox 100, Somerset, Rives BFK, Arches

SUGGESTED USES FOR DIFFERENT STRUCTURES

Display/Public Writing
Accordions, hanging scroll

Journal/Guest Book
Multiple signatures, chain stitch, slot and tab, pocket book, hand scroll

Photo Album/Scrapbook
Side-bound, ledger, concertina with tabs, chain stitch, flag book

Movable books that may suggest specific themes
Palm leaf, Venetian blind, scrolls, Jacob's ladder, tea bag books, piano hinge with skewers

Notepads
Perfect binding, ledger-style

Photo Display
Tunnel book, flag book, other accordion-fold books

Text *160–300 grams/square meter*
Books: accordion-fold books, tunnel book pages, palm leaf, Venetian blind, chain stitch (only 1–2 sheets per signature)
Suggested papers: Lenox 100, Arches, Rives BFK, Canson Mi Teintes, Stonehenge, Somerset Textured/Smooth
Text *90–115 grams/square meter*
Books: pocket book
Suggested papers: Rives Lightweight, Nideggan, German Ingres
Scrolls *40–60 grams/square meter*
Suggested papers: mulberry, Thai reversible Unryu, Thai Unryu, Yatsuo
Cover paper for softcover or pocket books *160–250 grams/square meter*
Suggested papers: Canson Mi Teintes, St. Armand, Indian Tea, other Indian papers, Fabriano Ingres Cover Heavyweight, Rives BFK, Stonehenge, Arches Cover, Lenox 100, Somerset, or other thick paper, double-sided (laminated) Thai Unryu paper
Paper portfolios *245–250 grams/square meter*
Suggested papers: medium–heavy weight, non-brittle: Indian sea, straw, jute; St. Armand, double-sided Thai Unryu paper (although lighter weight, it is strong), Larroque Mouchette
Cover paper for wrapped boards *130–250 grams/square meter*
Suggested papers: Canson Mi Teintes, St. Armand, Indian Tea, other Indian papers, Fabriano Ingres
Boards for hardcover books and Jacob's Ladder
Suggested papers: 4-ply museum board (100% rag, acid-free); 2 ply for small books, split board, or slipcase
Cover paper for hardcover book, box or portfolio *35–75 grams/square meter*
Suggested papers: any medium-weight Japanese paper or medium- to light-weight Western paper, book cloth, double-sided (laminated) Thai Unryu paper, light papyrus, German Ingres
Endsheets *35–160 grams/square meter*
Suggested papers: Yatsuo/Moriki, Canson, other light-weight (not sheer) decorative papers (darker colors probably work best, because they hide any of the outside covers' turn-ins)

Making Connections

As you create more books, you may find yourself with questions and wish to connect with others who share an interest in the book arts. The term "book arts" refers to a group of art techniques which include: bookbinding, calligraphy and lettering, paper marbling and decorations, letterpress printing, papermaking, and rubber-stamping, to name a few.

The book arts community is small but strong; many organizations around the world offer classes, lectures, and exhibits. Check for an organization in your area by looking in the telephone book under "Art Instruction." Also, inquire at universities in the art department or at the special collections department at the university or public library. Special collections librarians have a lot of information and should be able to direct you. Bookbinding supply and art supply stores often hold classes or have a bulletin board with classes listed. Look on the World Wide Web, too: book arts organizations now also have web sites. Just searching for "book arts" currently yields thousands of listings, so start by looking for one group (or one of the book artists listed in this book) and continue from there. A few specific organizations are: the Pacific Center for the Book Arts (San Francisco, but open to anyone, anywhere), the San Francisco Center for the Book, the Center for Book Arts (New York), Minnesota Center for Book Arts, Pyramid Atlantic (Maryland), and Columbia College Chicago Center for Book and Paper Arts.

Certain periodicals, such as the *Book Arts Classified,* based in Washington, D.C., can link you with organizations, resources, publications, classes, and book shows. Some of the groups have newsletters, calendars of events, and classes, and a quarterly publication (for a small membership fee).

A few art galleries/bookstores, mostly on the east and west coasts of the United States, in England, and in Germany, are solely devoted to selling book art. In these galleries you can not only view but hold and read many examples of fine and innovative bookwork. If the books have the address of the publisher, write to the artist. The book arts community is generally very open and friendly to inquiries.

Join an organization to receive current information about classes, exhibits, and new publications. Become active by volunteering your time. Then you can meet other bookmakers, show your work and get feedback, learn new techniques, and organize literacy-through-book-arts, art exchanges, or other programs. If you decide you are serious about selling your books, the group may provide a mailing list, teach you how to set up a business, or hold a book arts fair. Connect with the network.

Acknowledgments

I am grateful to the following people who contributed to this book: Betsy Davids, professor at California College of Arts and Crafts, who introduced me to the book arts, helped me to merge words and images, and supported me at every crossroads, Jim Hair, photographer, for his time and generosity; Nan Wishner, for editing the book's first draft; and Anne Schwartzburg and Val Simonetti, for proofreading the first draft and for their input and suggestions.

I am grateful to Nan and Betsy for asking the questions that helped make this a better book. I would also like to thank my editor at Sterling, Hannah Steinmetz, who encouraged me and made the revision process as entertaining as it was productive. Big thanks to the book "testers," who tried out some of my written instructions: Gina Covina, Linda Faber, Laurie Gordon, Trish Henry, Marie Mason, Peter McCormick, Claudia Moore, Val Simonetti, Karen Sjoholm, Melissa Slattery, Nan Wishner, and especially to Gina Lewis, who stayed all day!

I thank most of all my husband, Michael, who encouraged me to write this book, and my children, Mollie and Ezra.

About the Author

Alisa Golden has been making books under the imprint **never mind the press** since 1983. Her work is collected privately and by public libraries, universities, and museum libraries, including the New York Public Library; the Los Angeles Public Library; Wellesley, Brown, Harvard, and Yale; The Museum of Modern Art, New York; the San Francisco Museum of Modern Art; and the Victoria and Albert Museum, England. She has a Bachelor of Fine Arts in printmaking from the California College of Arts and Crafts in Oakland, California.